GW00771180

Waging war on woolly writing at work

Available on Amazon

Waging war on woolly writing at work

Jen Heggie

Copyright © 2015 Jen Heggie
All rights reserved.

ISBN: 1502977699
ISBN 13: 9781502977694
Library of Congress Control Number: 2015917181
CreateSpace Independent Publishing Platform
North Charleston, South Carolina

Contents

Why is this book needed?

There was a time, in living memory, when the people who wrote at work were almost always men. They would dictate the text which would then be typed up either by a secretary or by a member of the typing pool – the women. This was the era of typewriters and no self-respecting man would confess to being able to use one. The women who did the typing were trained in 'business language', how to present the text, punctuation and spelling and, with the writer, were responsible for making it perfect. The result would be popped in an envelope and sent off; the copies would head for the filing cabinet and the letters folder.

Then, in the sixties, along came computers and the sexual revolution. As computers developed, typewriters disappeared; typing skills became keyboard skills and the chaps took to it with gusto. Typing pools vanished and the role of secretary, where it still exists, has changed dramatically. Now, even chief executives and very senior managers, of both sexes, are expected to type their own communications. I sometimes wonder if this is the best use of their highly-paid time.

Email has added another dimension to this and these days just about everybody at work has to write. The assumption is that anyone who can use a keyboard can communicate in writing; the evidence tells us otherwise. Despite the fact that the number of people going on to universities and other tertiary education has increased enormously, the standard of written communication at work is poor. This is an expensive and time-consuming problem which this book addresses.

Who should read this?

Anyone who has to write in English at work, whether that be short internal emails, hefty reports, external communications to customers or clients, marketing or sales material – anything in writing related to work. Or anyone who employs or manages people who write on behalf of the organisation, who cares about the image conveyed by those written communications and who cares about the efficiency of the workforce.

Why?

Adopting the principles described in this book, will help you:

- save time and money – for you and those who read what you write
- become more efficient
- get your message across first time round
- enhance your reputation as a clear thinker and communicator
- be more confident in what you write
- probably improve your career prospects
- enjoy the process of writing

It's also short and to the point, in the spirit of the title.

What's this book about?

It's about what you write while you are at work, to help you get your message across to readers who:

- probably won't want to read it
- suffer from information overload
- are bored at even the prospect of reading

Don't under-estimate the fatigue that email and the internet causes; there's just too much to read. And most people read very inefficiently which makes it even more of a challenge to get the message across in writing. That's why the first section deals with how people read so you know what you're up against.

This has nothing to do with:

- academic writing – when you write to show off how much you know
- literature – when you write to entertain, enlighten, challenge or amuse
- journalism – when you write to fill the pages of an established print run

Nor has it anything to do with messaging, texting, twittering or social communication.

It's about showing respect for your readers by making sure that what you write is perfect: a clear message with no typos, no spelling mistakes, no grammatical errors. Because, make no mistake, at work, if you make mistakes in writing, people will notice and it will undermine your reputation. They'll notice the mistakes even if they can't write perfectly themselves – it's so unfair! People who recruit staff will routinely bin applications which contain errors; you may say that's unfair as well, but they have to adopt some criteria for rejecting applicants and an inability to write correct English is an easy one to spot.

This is about the activity when you invest your precious time putting words together in the hope that your readers will invest their precious time in reading them – and that they will understand the message first time round and do whatever you're asking of them. It's quite a tall order because of the writing process itself and because of the way most people read.

And it's about money

Whatever work you do, the way you use your time will affect your productivity. If you're self-employed, your productivity will translate directly into your profitability; if you work for someone else, whether in private or public service, it will contribute to the organisation's success. Increasingly, people at work write to each other, to their customers and to their suppliers. Computers and email have transformed working practices. The time you spend writing has to be put to good use if you're going to be successful.

Warning

My opinions on what constitutes good writing are, of course, subjective but they are firmly based on the primary purpose of writing at work – to get the message across. I take heart from eminent writers from the past like George Orwell, with whose opinions I usually agree, and contemporary commentators who eloquently mock pompous and jargon-laden writing. So we are not alone in this war on woolly writing.

What makes writing difficult? It's all down to the words. When you speak to someone face to face, you can reinforce your message with your body language and tone of voice. You can pick up their level of understanding by observing their reactions. On the phone, you can inject more meaning and emphasis through your voice, and they can participate in the conversation. Writing is a one-way activity; you don't know how the reader is interpreting the message, you don't know what else is going on at the time and you have no guarantee that they've read it all, or that they've read any of it.

On the face of it, writing is a poor way to communicate. But there are three huge advantages:

1. It's not spontaneous. You have time to think, plan, review, change and to make it perfect.
2. The recipient can't interrupt you while you're in full flow so you can write what you want to write without getting sidetracked.
3. It's there in black and white; good evidence that you've done something or if there's a dispute about what was said.

So let's exploit those advantages.

This book covers every aspect of writing at work.

- **Part one** covers everything you should know, or think about, before you start to write.
- **Part two** gives you some rules about how to express a clear message and find the right words, including how to get the best out of email and writing for an international audience.

- **Part three** covers the technical aspects to help you review what you've written and make it perfect: some tips on grammar, parts of speech and punctuation.
- **Exercises** are at the end so you can test yourself, your colleagues or family.

Part one: Before touching the keyboard

1. **How people read**

   The way we learn to read and the problems it causes, tips to help

2. **Think of the readers**

   Questions to ask before you start writing, empathy, seeing it from their point of view

3. **Planning what to write**

   Save time by planning, help your brain come up with ideas, mind mapping

4. **Creating the right structure**

   Hook the readers, feed them ideas so they can easily digest them, keep them reading to the end, paragraphs and headings

5. **Layout – how easy does it look to read?**

   First impressions matter, make it look easy

One

How people read

This might seem like an odd place to start but bear with me. If you understand how people read, you'll be able to see the process of writing from the reader's perspective. It might also help you become a better reader.

Why is reading a problem?
It comes down to the way most of us are taught to read: the letters of the alphabet, one at a time, combined to form words, read one at a time – and usually read aloud so the person who's teaching us can tell that we're pronouncing it correctly: a 'c' pronounced as 'k' as in cat, as opposed to an 's' as in circle. The whole process conspires to lock us into a reading speed that's not much faster than a speaking speed. The problem is called 'sub-vocalisation'.

Speaking and reading speeds are measured in words per minute (wpm). Most of us speak at about 150 to 200 wpm. People who sub-vocalise when they read don't read much faster than that – and that's a very slow reading speed. Trained readers can easily achieve speeds of 600-800 wpm. Think of the time that would save.

Sub-vocalisation means literally speaking the words to yourself as you read. Not out loud, of course – that's for kids. But most untrained adults believe they have to hear the words before they'll be able to understand them. You'll sometimes see even adults moving their lips as they read, particularly on the difficult words. You don't have to do this. The more you can reduce sub-vocalisation, the faster you'll be able to read.

Most sentences are a combination of key words – the ones that give us hard information – and supporting words to make it grammatical. You shouldn't give all the words equal attention; they don't deserve it. If you managed to restrict sub-vocalisation to just the key words, you'd make huge progress. It takes discipline to break yourself of the sub-vocalising habit but it makes a big difference. The two points that follow will help.

1) **Rhythm** Try to get into a rhythm when you read, moving your eyes steadily along the line from left to right. Untrained readers tend to allow their eyes to flit forwards and backwards, up and down, without even realising they're doing it. The phrase for it in reading jargon is '**involuntary regression**'. Re-reading words and feeding them to your brain in a jumbled order – no wonder it's so difficult to understand what you're reading.

   But we also indulge in **voluntary regression**. That's not quite as bad because at least we're conscious of doing it but it still slows us down. It's when you decide you need to read something again – a fact, a number, a paragraph, a page – because you're not confident it's gone in the first time. Try not to do this while you're reading a passage. You can always go back and read something again when you've read the whole thing, when you know what's important.

2) **Read in groups of words** This will really help because it stops you sub-vocalising and establishes a rhythm. The key words in a sentence are always surrounded by little words. And a writer always writes in phrases and sentences, not in single words at a time. So it makes sense to read words in groups. With practice, you can get really skilful at doing this; three or four words at a time, making use of punctuation. And if you read three words at a time, you can't possibly sub-vocalise them all so you'll automatically speed up.

Concentration Do you ever get frustrated by your seeming inability to concentrate when you're reading? Open plan offices don't help but we can all shut out noise and concentrate if we have the will to do so. Work reading isn't an automatic candidate for helping our concentration. But if you're reading at 200 wpm, it's no surprise that your brain is bored stiff and looking for something else to do. If you speed up your reading and read with purpose, you'll be better able to concentrate and you'll get more out of your reading.

So, the techniques you need to practise are to:

- read in groups of words
- put rhythm into your reading and cut out regression
- reduce sub-vocalisation

Remember – the emphasis here is on reading at work. Of course, if you want to read more newspapers or novels, these techniques will help. But non-work reading is a choice, an entertainment. Work reading is obligatory and it takes up time that could be spent doing something else. So the faster and more effectively we can get through it, the better.

Work reading isn't literature. True, some writers ramble and waffle but what they write could never be described as literature. We read at work to:

- get information
- decide what to do next
- improve our knowledge

And that's about it. So be ruthless about what you decide to read and be crystal clear why you're reading it if you decide to do so.

Preview the text before you start. Skim read, very quickly, the introduction, the first lines of each paragraph and the last paragraph. If it's written at all well, you should get the gist of what it's about.

- Do you need to read it? (delete or the bin is a good option)
- If you do decide to read it, be clear:
  - what are you expecting to get from it?
  - what will you do with the information?
  - where will it fit in your brain?
  - how much do you know about the subject already?
- Think before you start and practise your effective reading techniques when you read it.

Plan when you're going to read it. Reading requires more concentration than most activities at work so it makes sense to do it when you're feeling alert and bright. If you tend to fit in your work reading when you don't have other, more pressing, things to do, you'll end up reading when you're exhausted. It will take much, much longer.

It's good practice to set aside a session, morning and afternoon, for serious work reading. If you constantly dive into different activities at work, you make it hard to get the best out of your brain. Few of us are able to dictate exactly what we do at work, and when we do it, but most of us can plan a lot of it even if the plan sometimes gets hijacked by others. So plan your work reading, stick to it, practise the techniques and you'll be a much more effective reader.

We cover the use of mind maps for preparing to write in section 3; another use is to help you remember what you're read. If you're going to have to regurgitate the facts of what you've read, do a mind map of the key points. It works.

As you read the following sections on how to write clearly, remember how ineffectively your readers read. Your job is to make the message leap off the page, or screen, straight into your readers' heads despite their poor reading techniques.

Two

Think of the readers

Are you an expert? You probably are because that's what you're paid for. Whether that's a particular expertise in the workings of a procedure or some rare aspect of nuclear physics, your expertise is only useful if you can communicate it. Frequently you have to do that to people who don't share your expertise and you have to do it in writing. Your skill is to get the message across to people who don't have, and probably don't want to have, your in-depth knowledge. But they still need to use the information.

In the reader/writer relationship, it's your job as the writer to make the text as easy as possible to understand.

Before you start to write think about the readers. Allow your brain to flash through these questions.

Why   am I writing this? Is there a more effective way of getting the message across? Should I walk across the office and see them face to face? Would a phone call be easier? If the message is complicated or sensitive, seriously consider those options. You can always confirm the points from your conversation in writing afterwards.

If you decide to go ahead and write, think on.

Who   are the readers? What do they know already? Will they
       want to read it? Is English their first language? What
       do they think of me, my function, our organisation?
       The readers' perceptions are likely to colour their
       interpretation of your message.

What   do I want to achieve: to inform, pacify, persuade,
       influence, record? What do I want the reader to do as a
       result?

How   might the reader react? What sort of tone should I use?

When   will it be read? Will I be punished by posterity? Will
       people look back at my report in two years and find
       fault with my recommendations?

Where will it end up: in court, with a client, on the chief
       executive's desk, in the national press? Don't get
       paranoid about this but if you put something in writing,
       you lose control of it. That's particularly the case with
       email.

You might not have all the answers but the questions will help your brain
to focus and plan what to include.

Focus on the readers!

Three

Planning what to write

Yes. I am suggesting you turn away from your keyboard, and pick up a pencil and a blank sheet of paper because you will:

- produce a better piece of writing
- save time by getting it right first time

You don't have to do this for everything you write at work – sometimes a short email almost writes itself. But for anything which conveys several different ideas and requires you to think, this will really help.

Before the advent of computers, people either planned their writing or dictated their ideas as a first draft and edited, and edited, and edited. The cleverness of computers persuades us into thinking we can just get started – a heading here, a few words there. It's a slow and unsatisfactory way to write. This is why.

It's all to do with how our brains work. We can only concentrate on one thing at a time. You can't concentrate on thinking and writing at the same time. Thinking is about generating ideas and you can do that very quickly. Writing is about finding the right words to convey those ideas, making them coherent, putting them into grammatical sentences and communicating them in such a way that the reader understands it; it's a slower process but will be an awful lot quicker if you've done the thinking first.

We don't think logically. Our brains are very good at coming up with ideas, as long as they're not under too much pressure, but they don't do so in the right order. The great seduction of computers is that they have a delete button, and cut and paste. What bliss! No need to plan at all. Just tap out the words and move them around later. .... but if you've done that in the past and wondered why the process of writing was such a stop/start affair, that's the reason – you're paralysing your brain by asking it to do two things at once.

If you watch people writing at work, and maybe this applies to you too, you can see what happens. The moment they decide they have to write something, they lurch forward to the keyboard and make a start. In goes the address, the date, the greeting, maybe even the subject. They sit back and gaze at the screen with triumph; they've made a start, hooray! What next? Then it's forward again for the first sentence .... might that be a paragraph? Back to have a think. Then forward again for the next nugget. And so it goes on, in fits and starts. And if they're interrupted by a phone call mid sentence, the whole thing goes to pot. It's not an efficient use of time and it usually produces a mediocre piece of writing.

Please, help yourself think before you write. A technique like mind mapping is the most useful, and there's an example on the next page which is a mind map about the usefulness of mind maps which should help you get the idea. The principle is that you use key words to capture the ideas and that's enough to trigger your brain to come up with the rest. Tony Buzan is the person who came up with the original idea and has written many books on mind mapping and how we can help our brains work better. They're worth seeking out. Other people have adapted the principle and call them spidergrams or fish diagrams. You could even use a list – that would be better than nothing. But let me try and persuade you to use mind mapping.

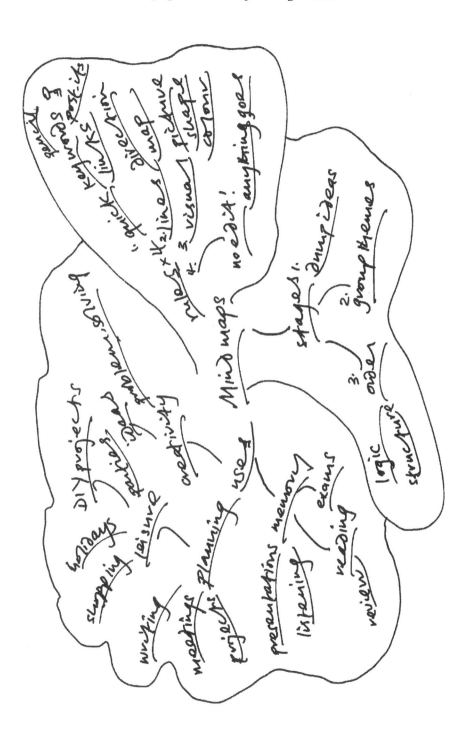

The rules of mind mapping are short and simple:

1. You want to capture your ideas quickly so you use key words only. No sentences, or phrases; abandon grammar and spelling – just get the words down. Allow your brain to come up with ideas that are associated. That's a natural reaction and it's where mind mapping differs from the concept of brainstorming.

2. Write along lines. It gives your ideas a sense of direction and if one idea is associated with another, link them so you start to build a structure. Don't worry too much about where to put the words. You can sort it out later. Use a pencil, with a rubber handy, or little post-its that you can move around.

3. Allow the words to build into a shape, a picture. Use colour if it helps. Use an image rather than words if it helps to stimulate your brain. Exploit your peripheral vision which works so much better in landscape than portrait.

4. Don't waste time debating whether an idea merits inclusion – just write it down. Chances are your brain has come up it with for a reason, and you can always reject it later.

So there we have it. 15 sentences, 188 words to convey to you, in grammatical English, what appears on the mind map as 18 key words for the section on rules. I've included on the mind map all their possible uses beyond simply helping you write well at work. I use them for every situation where thinking will help me complete the activity right first time and efficiently. And, yes, I even use them for the big shop at the supermarket. It doesn't stop some items spontaneously leaping off the shelves and finding themselves in my trolley. But it does mean I don't have to trawl up and down every aisle, and I do get everything I need.

Everything I've read about helping our brains work better suggests we need to clear the airwaves. Dump what's swirling around in your brain onto paper – or computer if you find that easier. If you don't, it's like the mental equivalent of dodgem cars, ideas crashing into each other – chaos. A big factor in reducing stress is to write it down: what's bothering you? what are the pros and cons? what should you do? what are the options? what do you need to discuss? Seeing a problem described and analysed on paper often serves to make it easier to solve.

Let's get back to using mind maps to write. Don't ask your brain to come up with ideas in the right order. That takes far too long and makes the task boring. The order in which you come up with the ideas doesn't matter. Down they go on to the page. You can group the ideas and sort out the order when you've finished generating them. Then it's very easy to think about the message, from the reader's point of view, and work out the logic and the structure.

Four

Creating the right structure

Now we need to think about structure. This is the order in which you present your ideas to the readers and it's all-important. If you get it right, you'll be able to hook your readers into actually reading it. Focus on the readers; what's most important from their point of view? Remember, your biggest challenge as a writer at work is getting people to start reading what you write. The way you structure your ideas will have a huge influence on persuading them to do this and to continue through to the end. After all, if they don't read it, you really are wasting your time.

Let's think about this from your point of view as a reader. How many emails do you get where the main point of it: 'please will you let me have the information by Friday' is buried in the last paragraph? Surely, the first thing you need to know is that you're being asked to do something by Friday; the why, the how and the wherefore of it can come later. The whole sense of it will fall into place if you read it knowing you have to produce some information.

This is what I mean by writing it from the readers' point of view. And this is why it's important to plan your ideas before you write – otherwise you'll be guilty of woolly writing by submitting the readers to your thought process. The great joy of writing is that you can think before you write.

Sorting out the structure is a bit like preparing a meal for a guest. We think about suitable food, what goes together well, quantities, recipes, timing. We want our guest to sniff the air with anticipation, tuck into the meal with gusto, finish it with a sigh of satisfaction and hopefully not suffer from indigestion, vomiting or worse. It's the same with writing. Just imagine your readers receiving your piece of writing and immediately thinking: 'This looks good. That's interesting. I need to know that and I need to do something about it.' They're hooked.

Do you need an executive summary? There's been a fashion for such things for a while but the need for it is an indictment of the structure. Such reports will be written like a scientific report: introduction, background, research and methodology, findings, conclusions, recommendations. The readers will be forced to read the thing from the writer's point of view, and the writer is probably showing off how much work s/he's done. Readers don't want to do that. The reason the writer gets paid is to come up with recommendations – let's hear about them upfront. Of course, sensible readers will skip to the recommendations first and probably ignore the rest, but why don't the writers write it like that in the first place?

As an example of the difference between a thinking structure and a writing structure, let's take a report that's making a proposal to sort out a problem – a very typical reason why people write reports. A perfect way to think and plan the report would be to do a mind map around the five Ps:

- Purpose: why I've been asked to look into this
- Position: what's the current position
- Problem: what's the problem with the current position

- Possibilities: what are the options for dealing with it
- Proposal: which do I think is the best option

That would be a very logical way to think about what should go into the report. But it wouldn't be a great way to write it because the reader has to wait until the end to learn of your proposal – the most important feature. The written structure would have far more impact if it were:

1. Purpose: a brief paragraph to set the scene
2. Proposal: this is what I suggest
3. Problem: this is how it would sort out the problem
4. Position: this was the current position
5. Possibilities: these were the other options I considered, and rejected

Now, if the readers are in a real hurry, it won't take them long to see what you're proposing. And if they agree (or have such total trust in you), they won't have to go beyond point 2. If they do decide to read on, the way you've written it will hook them by answering the questions that your structure will create in their minds:

(Why am I reading this?)
   1. Purpose: a brief paragraph to set the scene
(What am I being asked to agree to?)
   2. Proposal: this is what I suggest
(Why was this a problem? What's the context?)
   3. Problem: this is the problem it will resolve
(What's wrong with the current position?)
   4. Position: this was the current position
(Did you think about any other options?)
   5. Possibilities: these were the other options
      I considered, and rejected

The structure employed by journalists works well: a headline to grab the attention, the first two or three sentences with hard hitting facts and then the rest. I'm not suggesting you write like journalists; they're paid to fill the pages and their readers choose to pay to read them. But the structure will help your readers at work get the important facts as fast as possible without unnecessary embellishment.

There's no single structure that works well in all circumstances but the principle is to present whatever you're writing in the order that makes the best sense to your readers.

Where do you mention money? If you're writing about something that involves money – either spending it or saving it – put the amount upfront as speedily as possible, maybe even in the heading. Readers are interested in money – it focuses the brain. And it starts them asking questions:

- Why do we need to spend that amount?
- What will it do for us?
- What will happen if we don't invest?
- Could we do it cheaper?

There's the embryo of your structure.

Focus on the main story. Don't dilute the power of your message with unnecessary details, facts or research; you can always put those in an annexe if you need to include them. Don't forget, at work, if your readers need more information, they can usually ask.

Use headings to help your readers navigate the page, interesting ones that make them want to read on. 'Introduction' always strikes me as one of the most boring, and self-evident, of headings, hotly followed by 'Conclusion'. You can do better than that!

We can learn from the world of marketing – appropriately, because when you're writing at work, you're marketing ideas, trying to influence. Marketing leaflets often adopt the question and answer technique – the question as the heading and the answer as the information below it. It's a good way to get into your reader's brain and involve them with the text.

As a link to the discussion on mind mapping, you'll find it helpful to generate headings at the mind map stage, and this will help you plan the structure.

Paragraphs This is how you graphically present your structure to the readers: chunks of information for them to digest. Paragraphing is very important. Giving your readers a paragraph – a piece of text surrounded by white space, helps the text to stand out and makes it look easier to read. Paragraphs are part of the layout and this will contribute to the reader's decision about whether or not to read it.

There are three points to remember about paragraphs:

> **A paragraph is a theme** - a cluster of related sentences. Separate the themes into paragraphs and the reader will be able to follow the flow. The double space between paragraphs creates the wonderful chunk of blankness that says: "We've finished with that theme; now we're moving on to the next." Don't explain more than one theme in each paragraph.

Paragraphs shouldn't have more than six sentences. That might sound somewhat arbitrary – but if you're ever read Dickens, you'll sympathise with the argument. If the paragraphs are long and dense, your readers will very soon get confused and give up. Short paragraphs mean you're not asking your reader to concentrate for too long without a breathing space.

Sometimes a one sentence paragraph is very effective at grabbing the reader's attention to make a key point.

Every paragraph should begin with a brief statement of its theme. This 'topic sentence' acts as a signpost to help the reader; it shouldn't be more than 15 words. Your readers should be able to get the gist of your message by skim reading the signpost sentence of each paragraph. That's what efficient readers do to preview a document to help them decide how closely they need to read it – or if they need to read it at all. It's a great discipline for you as a writer because it forces you to identify what's important.

Under the section on **Tips to help you write clearly**, we'll cover sentences and the number of words you should aim for; that will affect the density of words contained in your paragraphs.

Now let's turn to first impressions and layout.

Five

Layout – how easy does it look to read?

O ur face to face interactions are heavily influenced by first impressions. So it is with writing. If the text looks easy to read, your readers are more likely to make a start. We've already discussed the importance of paragraphs, presenting the information in thematic chunks with space all around. Here are ten other points to make the layout of your text work in your favour.

1. **Have generous margins**. Don't ask your readers to spend too long on the same line. Reports presented in landscape may be original but they're hard work because the line of words is unusually long. And if the text is in columns, it's a bore if you're reading it on a screen, having to scroll up and down.

2. **Block layout** Everything – including headings – starts from the left, except when you're indenting sub-paragraphs. This is logical because we read from left to right.

3. **Avoid total justification** Total justification is when both the left and right margins are in straight vertical lines. A lot of people like the neatness of this.........but we're not interested in neatness,

we're interested in readability. There are two very good reasons why you should avoid total justification:

- It makes the text shapeless. It's more difficult to read because of this, and more difficult for the readers to identify which line they're on. This is particularly important in a long letter or report.

- It creates arbitrary spaces within the line because the text has to be stretched to reach the right margin. This undermines the influence of typography – see 5. below – and reduces readability. (This paragraph is fully justified, as an example. Looks funny, doesn't it?)

4. **No punctuation in addresses or abbreviations** We used to scatter full stops and commas around the text with gusto; the fashion now is to use punctuation only when it helps the reader understand the content.

So no full stops after: Mr plc CMC Ltd eg ie
No commas after Dear Fred or Yours sincerely
No commas in lines of address:

Ms J A Thomson
2 Walcot Parade
Reading
RG1 5NF

5. **Dates** Write out dates in full at the top of a letter and within the text. Abbreviated dates like 14/2/09, or 19-5-12 look messy, and confusing if there are other numbers on the page. It's also potentially confusing if your readers are used to the American way of writing dates, with the month first; 9/11 is 11September, not 9 November. Current convention suggests you leave out *the*

before the date: *We wrote to you on the 4th July* should now be written *We wrote to you on 4ᵗʰ July.*

6. **Typography matters!** Don't laugh; this is to do with helping your readers breathe and, if they're untrained readers, they'll certainly be sub-vocalising. We discuss punctuation in section 14 but for now, the convention is:

    two spaces after a full stop, a question mark and an exclamation mark, followed by a capital letter; this gives your readers time to take a deep breath before starting on the next sentence

    one space after a comma, semicolon and colon, and one space either side of a dash; it's the same key on the keyboard but the space either side elongates it – to distinguish it from a hyphen -

    no spaces either side of a hyphen or a slash mark

7. **Avoid using capitals for words.**

    WE MUST HAVE A REPLY BY NEXT FRIDAY AT THE VERY LATEST. IF WE DO NOT HEAR FROM YOU WE WILL ASSUME WE HAVE THE GO-AHEAD.

    In email language, capitalising words is known as shouting and tends to be frowned upon. But capitalised words also reduce readability; they're more difficult to recognise because they have no shape. Motorway signs, for instance, are in lower case. If you were bowling up the M6 and passed a sign for MANCHESTER or MACCLESFIELD, it would be far more difficult to distinguish, at speed, than Manchester or Macclesfield. Avoid underlining for the same reason.

We had to resort to capitalised headings, or underlining, when all we had were typewriters. Those days are long gone and our computers offer us far more flexibility. Use bold, italics, colour or change the font size instead. If I'm writing a report, I tend to use font 16 for titles, font 14 for headings and font 12 bold for sub headings. Make sure you're consistent and don't go mad with a confusing array of fonts and colours; the font of your heading is a subtle way of reinforcing its status; is this a major heading or a sub heading?

8. **Use bullet points** to help your message leap off the page. We've already discussed the importance of white space. The sensible use of bullet points can shorten the text and make it easy for your readers. But endless lists can be very tedious; you need to inject a narrative to keep your readers interested.

Bullet points can also help avoid repetition by putting the controlling verb in the main sentence. For example:

Following the rules in this book will help you:
- write clearly and concisely
- have impact on your readers
- use correct grammar and punctuation
- exercise more influence through written communication
- save time when writing

The controlling verb is 'will help'; it would be very tedious to repeat it five times.

Make sure you don't undermine the benefit of bullet points by using woolly language. If you're itemising a list of, say, six options, introduce it by saying: 'We looked at six options' not 'We looked at a number of options'; that just makes it sound as if you're making it up as you go along.

9. **Use headings** – good ones, to help readers see the picture. We touched on headings under structure, stressing the importance of making your headings work for you to get the message across. A heading is like a headline in a newspaper, a few words writ large to catch your attention. Your choice of newspaper will dictate the likely usefulness of the heading; your job at work is to come up with headings that give your readers an inkling of what's to come and attract them to start reading. So rather than **Recommendations** as a heading why not **How can we tackle this?**

    Headings are useful no matter what you're writing. They're just as relevant in an email or letter as they are in a report.

10. **Use graphs, diagrams, pictures, cartoons** to enhance the message. *A picture speaks a thousand words* is the saying; a well-chosen image can indeed take the place of, perhaps not a thousand words, but quite a few – and it might entertain your readers as well as educate them. But don't just bung in graphics for the sake of a bit of colour – they have to be relevant and meaningful to the readers, and contribute to your message.

Before we leave this section, a note of caution. Computers enable us to do all sorts of fancy stuff: changing the font, introducing colour, boxing in bits of text, changing the background colour............Two points:

- I've edited documents where for reasons of, who knows, originality? we've had white text against a pale green background. Why? It's really difficult to read even though it might look quite pretty from a distance. The reason we generally have black print against a pale, usually white, background is that it's easy to read. And that should be the priority.

> - Then there are bits of boxed text. I've never read any scientific analysis of graphics and layout so my comment on this is entirely subjective. When I see text that has been boxed in, my tendency is to skip it. It doesn't leap out at me begging to be read; it stays in its box sulking at being ignored. So I hope you've read this.

But some people love boxes and use them for examples or illustrations, or for witty quotations. The choice is yours; if it works for you, it will probably work for the readers.

Part two: Getting down to writing

Six

Tips to help you write clearly

You're trying to convey a message in writing and usually words are all you can use. They look exactly the same as the words in all the other messages your readers are expected to read that day; if you want them to read your message, make it easy for them.

The writer, George Orwell, who was acknowledged as a great thinker as well as a writer, was an enthusiastic advocate of clear writing – and he died in 1947. His seven golden rules are just as relevant now as they were then. Here they are as a checklist; we look at some points in more detail later.

1.   **Write as you would speak** That isn't an invitation to use verbal mannerisms, slang or ungrammatical language but an encouragement to use the main words you would speak; simple, straightforward language. Speaking is a spontaneous activity and most of us use everyday language that immediately springs to mind.

As we said earlier, one of the advantages of writing is that you have time to think but this becomes a hefty disadvantage if you use that time to come up with over-clever, pompous language, the sort of words you were encouraged to use in academic life which made you sound intelligent. You've left academic life and your job now is to communicate; to **express** not **impress**. For example:

instead of	use	instead of	use
assistance	help	endeavour	try
regarding	about	comprehend	know
discontinue	stop	commence	start
intelligible	clear	make modification to	modify, change
demonstrate	show	proceed	go

The words you use are so important, we come back to them in the next section – Finding the right words.

Think **A B C**: accurate, brief and clear. That sounds easy enough, doesn't it?

2.   **Never use a long word if a short one will do** A long word is one with three syllables or more (syllable has three syll-a-bles). It's not to do with the number of letters in the word, it's the way we speak or hear it. So id-e-a-lly is a long word as it has four syllables. Trans-formed is a short word because it only has two. Long words take longer to read and your readers may not understand them. Their use may also make you sound over-formal and pompous. This relates to the clarity index explained at the end of this chapter.

3.   **If it's possible to cut out a word, always cut it out** The more words you use to convey your message, the more chance your message will be diluted. So get to the point with the least delay. Quantity doesn't equal quality; in writing, less is more.

example: If we were to co-sponsor with them this
could significantly and cost effectively assist
our publicity in the Middle East also.

why not: Co-sponsorship would also be a low cost way of
boosting our publicity in the Middle East.

**4.   Never use a foreign phrase, a technical word or a jargon word
if you can think of an everyday English equivalent** Acronyms are OK
if everyone easily understands them but don't use them to mystify or
impress. Always write out the acronym in full the first time you use it
even if you think all your readers know it. Jargon can be very tedious so
keep it to a minimum (see the next chapter) And please don't use Latin!
Eg and ie are OK but avoid *inter alia (amongst others or other things), via
(by, through), viz (namely, in other words, that is to say).* I don't know why
we still use 'per annum' when 'a year' means the same. There's no point
in being brief if your readers have difficulty understanding it.

Remember, the mark of a true expert is someone who can convey his/her
expertise in language that people who don't share their expertise can easily understand.

5.   Avoid stock phrases These are phrases like 'Please do not hesitate
to contact us if you have any further queries' which suggest a robot has
written the letter; they don't convey sincerity and do nothing to build
rapport with the reader. This is especially important when you're writing
to customers. See chapter 9 Building rapport with the reader.

6.   Never use the passive voice when you can use the active voice
Grammar-check is jolly useful, not so much in offering a correction but
in highlighting a possible mistake; it's asking '*do you really want to put*

that?' So when you get a squiggly green line under the text, it's telling you that you're writing in the **passive** voice – and everything that's been written on the subject of writing clearly suggests you should write, most of the time, in the **active** voice. This mystifies many so here's what it means. (There's more on this in section 12 Grammar and an exercise in section 17.)

A sentence must have a subject (what the sentence is about) and a verb (the doing word), and the subject is usually at the beginning of the sentence.

In the active voice the subject is **doing** the activity of the verb:

The cat scratched the dog

In the passive voice the subject is **receiving** the activity of the verb

The dog was scratched by the cat

You'll notice that the passive voice is longer and the reader has to get to the end of the sentence to find out who/what did it. Of course, you could shorten it by leaving out *by the cat* but then the reader misses a vital piece of information.

It doesn't matter so much in a short and trivial sentence but how about this:

Regional delivery of the staged review of consents process has not been comprehensively ground-truthed by combination region/area plans, and it is therefore unclear as to whether sufficient resource has yet been committed to the process to achieve the necessary outcomes by the inherent national deadlines.

Phew! I think this means:

Regions haven't yet checked that they have committed sufficient resources to enable them to review the stages of the consents process within the national deadlines.

The passive voice isn't wrong, and scientists are told to use it throughout their academic careers; this is because the nature of science is that it should be objective and impersonal. But it tends to deaden the text and make it dull. Here's another example:

This has been replaced by the item being weighed and a price calculated by the mail room staff who then place the required price of the stamp on the item by way of the franking machine.

That's 36 words to say:

Mail room staff now weigh the item, calculate the price and frank it.

Also, we rarely speak in the passive voice. If you're writing to communicate, try to use the active voice.

7.   **Never write a sentence longer than 40 words and keep your average sentence length to 20 words or fewer** This is to do with how we read and breathe; as we've already discussed, most untrained readers believe they have to hear the word to understand it – *sub-vocalisation*. We rarely speak in sentences of more than 20 words for the simple reason that we run out of breath. The same thing happens when we have to read long sentences: the message is simply indigestible. Try reading this one out loud:

We believe that our proposals in terms of service delivery with our focus on patient delivery using our a+ brand for cleaning and our proposed refurbishment of the catering facility to further enhance the Trust's reputation to be best in class will ensure that our proposed services meet your values, maintaining your low infection rates with increased supervision working to achieve excellent PEAT scores. (64 words)

Vary the length of sentences to keep life interesting for the reader but keep the average length to 20 words. And remember: a sentence is one unit of thought, an idea. We come back to this in section 14 on Punctuation.

To conclude, these rules are all about writing clearly and making your messages more readable, based on the evidence of how untrained readers read, as we discussed in part 1. There is consensus here; readability scores exist which are based on the average number of:

- syllables in each word
- words in each sentence

You can find them, and apply them, through your computer but I think they're rather over-complicated and confusing. Instead I offer you the clarity index.

Clarity index

This is based on the:

- average number of words in each sentence, and to calculate this you include the six major punctuation marks . ? ! : ; – plus
- percentage of long words – that is, words with three syllables or more

You ignore headings and proper nouns, names like Miliband, Cameron, Professor, Minister, Commission.

If your average sentence length is 20 words and your percentage of long words is 10, you end up with a clarity index of 30. If you reduce your average sentence length to 15 and your percentage of long words to 5, you end up with a clarity index of 20. It's a question of style and the daily newspapers are excellent exponents of it.

Journalists know exactly what their editors expect of them. Each of the daily newspapers will have a precise profile of their readership; the style of writing they adopt – and the pictures and headlines – will match the readers' expectations.

Compare these two editorials from The Sun and The Daily Telegraph.

1 Flood of tears

The storms may be over – but the **legacy** of the floods will be with us for weeks. Thousands have suffered. But **mercifully** few have paid such a price as Helen Swinstead, whose husband died as their cruise ship was battered by gales. Brave Helen says James will be sitting on a cloud chortling "because he's never made headlines before". Her courage is an **example** to us all.

This is 67 words with 6 major punctuation marks so the average sentence length is 11 + percentage of long words $\frac{3}{67}$ x 100 = 4.4%, let's call it 4%.

This has a clarity index of 15.

2 Mr Miliband's climate lectures ring hollow

..........A balance has to be struck between **conservation** and **economic** growth, and Mr Miliband's **radical** approach to the former could have a **deleterious** effect upon the latter. He backs **hopelessly ambitious emissions** targets and the **expansion** of wind power, which, **ironically**, is so **inefficient** that it can often require the use of **polluting** backup. It has also been financed by **subsidies** that come straight out of the **consumers**' pockets. Making our power supplies **costlier** and less **reliable** will do little to curb global warming, but it will make life more **miserable**.

Mr Miliband has a canny **ability** to **identify** people's concerns and to exploit **apparent** Government **confusion** or **inactivity**. But his **solutions** are almost **inevitably** wrong. ....

This has 116 words and 6 major punctuation marks so the average sentence length is 19. There are 23 long words so the percentage is 23 x 100 = 20%
                                                                                                        116

This has a clarity index of 39.

The first is The Sun, the second The Daily Telegraph. It's worth remembering that The Sun is by far the most popular newspaper in Britain with a circulation of more than 2.2 million. That's just the people who buy it; estimates of its readership are three times that many. The Daily Telegraph sells about 557,500.

The point about the clarity index is that you don't really need to calculate it; at a glance you can see that the extract from The Sun is easier to read than the one from The Daily Telegraph, even without identifying the long words in bold. And there's no right or wrong; it's a question of style but that style should be geared to your readers' expectations. Your readers at work don't buy your communications as they do a newspaper, out of choice for entertainment. It's probably unwise to indulge in Sun-speak but it all depends.

As a rough guide, I suggest you aim for a clarity index of 20-25 for emails and 30-35 for reports, proposals, business cases. If you're writing about a subject that is itself a long word – let's say 'economic development' – and you have to include words like financial, subsidies, taxation and government, you probably need to keep your sentences short and use bullet points to help reduce the clarity index.

Seven

Finding the right words

For this subject, in particular, I want you to remember what you feel like as a reader. How do other writers' words affect you? What type of language persuades you to read on? You can be sure that your readers will share your preferences. Let's also remember that we're writing to communicate; we're not talking about literature or academic writing, nor about newspapers or magazines.

Your relationship with your readers is this: you're asking them to invest their precious time in reading your words. The onus is on you to balance the equation by making sure that every word is precious to the readers. Let's think of your words as jewels that you're offering to them; their value will be measured by the extent to which they achieve what you're trying to do – inform, record, persuade, influence, maybe even entertain. At the very least, you want the readers to read and understand them.

How tolerant are you as a reader? Most readers at work find it easy to give up; unless it's well-written, boredom strikes and they lose concentration. Few readers will bother to re-read a sentence that isn't immediately understandable. So you have to use words that convey your message, accurately, first time round, and that keep the readers' interest.

Are we talking about dumbing down? NO! Even the wonderful George Orwell suggests using short words if they're available. Simple language isn't simplistic. We're using language to express a message, not to impress the readers with the extent of our vocabulary.

I love learning new words. I love the fact that our language has such a variety of words, and some so particular. How about 'uxorious'? It means: 'greatly or excessively fond of one's wife'. Watch out, ladies! I enjoy reading books and articles that force me to consult the well-thumbed dictionary. The English language is a marvel but we're more likely to get our messages across successfully at work by using everyday language that we would readily speak.

I accept that language, particularly the English language which is used so widely around the world, changes and develops. We introduce new words and phrases; a dictionary is a little out of date as soon as it goes into print. But the basis of communication is that we have a shared understanding of what the words mean and we need to use those words as precisely as we can. A lack of precision leads to ambiguity and misunderstanding and, at the very least, it wastes time.

Do you remember the events leading up to the American/British invasion of Iraq in 2003? There was a UN Security Council Resolution 1441, the wording of which was agreed after much wrangling. When push came to shove, and America and Britain decided to invade, they invoked Resolution 1441 to justify the action. Other countries, France, China and Russia in particular, invoked the very same Resolution to condemn the invasion as illegal. I'm not a diplomat, but it's hard to understand how words could be so tragically and ambiguously interpreted.

A more recent example, February 2015, is a quote from Nato's deputy supreme allied commander in Europe: "The threat from Russia, and the risk it brings of miscalculation resulting in a strategic conflict, represents an existential threat to our whole being." I think he means: 'Russia is a major threat and we need to do something about it.'

For most of us, our writing doesn't have such a wide-ranging influence but the principle remains the same: we should use words that our readers will easily understand and interpret in the way that we intend. Even that is quite a challenge if you're writing to a multi-national audience. See chapter 11 for more on this.

I hate the way our language is tortured by writers at work who over-use bland boring words that convey neither precision nor interest. I call it blancmange writing. If you love blancmange, this analogy might not work for you.

Why blancmange? To me, blancmange is a big disappointment; it looks quite promising from a distance, it has presence, it looks solid. But, the minute you cut into it, it starts wobbling. Getting it onto your plate and into your mouth can be hazardous and, once there, there's nothing to bite on; it just slides down your throat – like invalid food. Deeply unsatisfactory.

A lot of the documents I'm asked to edit fall into the category of blancmange writing. They purport to be interesting text, frequently with coloured graphics to spice things up but, the minute I start to read, I'm overwhelmed by a wave of boredom and frustration. At least I'm getting paid to edit, so that keeps me going! The problem is that the writers over-use words like:

Issue/s, and frequently **'key issue/s'** It's such a lazy word. What information does it give me as a reader? Is it good or bad? I need some clues to know how to react, to know where to put the information in my brain. Our language has so many more precise words to convey what I should be feeling: problem, question, disaster, concern, worry, subject, topic, point, area.......

Stakeholders It's a perfectly good word and should refer to those who have an identified vested interest in the subject. To broaden its use to include, as politicians and others do, just about everyone simply undermines the power of its meaning; to talk about 'stakeholders in the NHS' is meaningless when in fact it means the whole population.

Sustainable, sustainability They've both become vogue words over the last ten years with our concerns over the natural environment and man's impact on it. The meaning behind sustainable is that it has to have the potential to self-regenerate; so to talk about a sustainable approach to forestry is fine. But it's another word that's been hijacked to add gravitas (another word favoured by politicians) and is used instead of permanent, long term, durable, lasting. For the Minister of Defence to talk about the sustainability of sending troops into Afghanistan is nonsense.

Transparent, transparency It's funny how words get adopted; politicians use them, the media reports it and bingo! everyone's at it. If I described you as transparent, you would be insulted; it means 'easily seen through, obvious'. I see what politicians are trying to convey: "Hey, we have nothing to hide" but they transparently do hide things so the more they use the words, the less likely we are to believe them. If they were transparent, they wouldn't need to talk about it. And whatever happened to the words 'open' and 'honest'? We all know what they mean.

Then the words get taken up by business and we get 'transparent accounting' and other transparencies. I would be more impressed by "You'll have access to all accounts online" – it's longer but at least I know what I'm getting.

Partnership What a cosy relationship that implies – equality, balance, mutual interest, shared values, common goals. In most cases, it's more honest simply to say 'We work with........' For a supermarket to market itself on the grounds that 'we work in partnership with our suppliers' is a hoot; most suppliers would say that their margins are squeezed and the supermarket is a ruthless tyrant, out to make as much money as possible at their expense.

What does 'in partnership' add? "We work in partnership with community groups." "We work with community groups." Is there a difference?

Significant, substantial Classic blancmange words! I accept the use of 'significant' in a mathematical or scientific context. I don't accept it for general use in any other context. 'We've made significant/substantial progress.' What a useless sentence! 'We've achieved three of our four main goals, namely ....' Now that tells the readers something and they can decide whether or not that merits the adjective 'significant'.

Effective, effectively Again, their use is usually meaningless. 'We need to effectively improve our approach to marketing.' a) You could hardly improve ineffectively; b) improve means to get better at doing something; c) the reader would be far more enlightened by: "We need to market ourselves better by doing XYZ." If you look at any sentence which includes effective or effectively, you can almost always leave it out without any loss of meaning.

Several, a number of Now this really sounds as if you're making it up as you go along. Be specific! Help the reader anticipate and make sense of what you're writing:

- Three points stand out ....
- Two areas in particular need attention .....
- We have four concerns about this project......

and then go on to itemise them.

On a regular basis ???? That could be once a day, once a week, once a month, once a year ....There's no point in writing it, particularly if it's attached to the word 'monitor' which means 'to maintain regular surveillance over'. Stick your head over the parapet and commit yourself: 'We'll check the pumping station each Thursday.' 'Each year, an engineer will inspect the installation.'

Qualified, competent I almost put 'qualified engineer' in the sentence above but managed to stop myself. There's no point in putting either word, unless you're referring to the legal term 'competent authority'. Would you suggest using an unqualified or incompetent person to do something? I think not. Surely the reader has the right to assume a level of competence; neither 'qualified' nor 'competent' adds anything to the meaning.

Specific This is another word that has crept into business writing and is usually not required. 'This is a problem specific to the creative department' would be fine as a way of defining the problem, but you could just as easily put 'Only the creative department has this problem.'

Strategy, strategic These two should apply to a timeframe of at least three years or to a complex plan, as in a military strategy. People use it to inflate the importance of what they're proposing and it misfires; there's nothing wrong with a plan, task or action.

Deliver, delivery, deliverable Let's keep those words – the first two at least – to what the postal service does. We give or provide a service, we achieve results (or outcomes, if you must), our service is excellent – you don't need to put service delivery; service has to be something you do to, or for, others. A document that has just appeared on my desk includes this paragraph:

What will be delivered?
The investments will deliver:

- Restoration of the internal paths and landscape
- Refurbishing of the benches
- Re-instatement of the historic east and west gateways
- Enhanced boules squares
- Enabling of temporary road closures for events
- Improvements for pedestrians and cyclists

It would be much more direct to write

With this investment we will:

- restore the paths and landscape
- smarten up the benches
- re-instate the east and west gateways
- re-lay the boules squares
- enable road closures for events
- improve access for pedestrians and cyclists

Develop further Leave out 'further'; the word develop already has the sense of progress.

Currently Unless you really want to stress that something is happening now (so why not use 'now'?), leave it out. The tense of the verb already indicates the present, as in: 'We're currently experiencing problems.......' means exactly the same as 'We're experiencing problems ....'

Quality assured It came into vogue about twenty years ago under the Total Quality Management (TQM) banner and, sadly, it stayed. You can only use this expression if you have a well-defined yardstick or measure against which you can assess the action. Don't use it if what you're doing is checking, assessing, reviewing or evaluating.

Continuous improvement comes from the same TQM stable and it's very tired. It's inconceivable that anyone would try not to improve – at least they'd never admit it – so find a more sincere way of conveying the message. 'Each month, we'll review what we've achieved and identify how we can improve.'

Innovative, innovation Words much loved by sales teams to try and persuade potential clients of their creativity. If you've designed the first bagless vacuum cleaner, that's innovation. If you're describing your approach to recruitment, training, cleaning, teamworking, charging – it's not innovative; it's new, different, unusual. Or why not just describe it and let the reader decide? Don't over-sell; it doesn't work.

Direction of travel as in 'We are working closely with the strategic alignment team and others to maintain an understanding and help shape the direction of travel and solutions that are both fit for the future network and for ourselves.' This has probably taken over from 'the route map' and 'the journey'. It's all pretty nasty. I'd prefer: 'We're working closely with the strategic alignment team and others to understand their positions and develop solutions that suit both their needs and ours.'

Those are my chief contenders for blancmange writing; there are more and you could probably add some of your favourites. In brief, the message is this:

- You can probably get away with using any one of those words above, occasionally; if you pepper your text with them, the readers will give up.

- Have you noticed how almost all of them count as long words, in line with George Orwell's definition – three syllables or more? So it's a double whammy; they all contribute to raising the clarity index, making the text more difficult to read and they add very little, if anything, to the meaning.
- Under section 6, Tips to help you write clearly, rule 2 says use short words rather than long ones. Rule 3 says if you can cut out a word, always do so; the more words you use, the more your message will be diluted.
- Use strong language and commit yourself! Hedging your bets by using wishy-washy language doesn't work. The readers can see through it and will just get irritated by your lack of conviction. If you can't tell it how it is, don't write anything.

How about this for a classic example of blancmange writing:

Our existing reputation for effective delivery in a complex and rapidly changing environment, alongside a thorough understanding of the sector with its economic and legislative drivers, and the added value of established networks and internal support structures creates a uniquely strong partnership drawing on both generic and sector specific skills and experience.

I'm not making it up. That was from a sales proposal............and they didn't get the contract.

Jargon, management-speak or shall we just call it bullshit? We can't leave the section on language without discussing this. There used to be a game, popular for spicing up meetings, called Bullshit Bingo; there was a card with all the hackneyed words and phrases and when each had been used at least once during the meeting........ bingo! Harmless fun and it kept people awake but there's a serious side to it. The card included:

Key issue/s
Strategy
Stakeholders
Blue sky thinking
Value-added
Thinking outside the box
Continuous improvement
Partnership
Touch base
Push the peanut

No, I'm not sure what the last one meant either. At least at a meeting, you could ask the speakers to explain exactly what they meant. Not that anyone did, for fear of looking foolish and outside the circle. The result of using such words is a wave of incomprehension and irritation.

It's even worse in writing when the readers are left to work out the meaning for themselves. Our language has a wonderful word to describe exactly this: obfuscate. It means to obscure, confuse, stupefy, bewilder. It can be a verb – obfuscate; a noun – obfuscation; and an adjective – obfuscatory. So we can all join in a chorus of

Down with obfuscation!

I've done a lot of work with sales teams who have to write proposals to get business. When I suggest they're writing less than clearly, they often respond that they're trying to leave themselves 'wriggle room'. I always respond that it will irritate the potential client, who will easily see through the tactic, and probably lose them the business at stage one. It doesn't convey honesty and it wastes time. And if they did get the contract, the lack of clarity in the proposal would end up causing a huge problem at the contract stage.

I've always thought the legal term 'beyond all reasonable doubt' is asking for trouble but let's not open the Pandora's box that is our legal system.

I'm not closed to new words or phrases entering our language – it is a living entity – but their use can become very tedious. It's like seeing an ad on TV that's really clever the first time you see it; second time, it's OK but by the third, you're bored. Pity the poor advertisers!

'Going forward' was one of the more irritating phrases of Blair's government – as if we don't have a future tense. And 'let me just say this........' as a prelude to any response. We know it's a way to buy thinking time but it wastes our listening time. Your job as a writer is to invest your time in finding the right words to save the readers' time.

How about this as an introduction to a document:

By working together and streamlining our approach we will deliver a step change in the way we deliver that ensures we are fit for the future by reducing the overall cost and improving our effectiveness by developing and fully utilising the skills of our people, and ensuring we extract the maximum from the evidence we collect and that which we can access from others.

Blah, blah ......

A final point, just in case you're still unconvinced of the folly of using obfuscatory language. In 2002 KPMG, one of the big six accountancy firms, reviewed the annual reports of major companies. This was during the time of the spectacular collapses of Enron, WorldCom and others. They found a clear link between obfuscation in the annual report and the likely demise of the company. I rest my case.

Eight

Cutting out the excess words

Our language has a word 'tautology' which has two meanings:

1. When you say the same thing twice over in different words; the example in the dictionary is: 'arrived one after the other in succession'

2. A statement that is necessarily true: 'All Labour supporters are slightly left wing.'

I'm mostly concerned about the first meaning. When we speak, we get away with using tautologies and excess words because we're having to think and express ourselves at the same time, and the excess words will probably just wash over the listeners like a wave. But, as we've already discussed, the huge advantage of writing over speaking is that it's not spontaneous; you can cut out words that don't add to the meaning. That being the case, you must do it.

Here are some of my favourite examples; some are tautologies, others are just excess words – the words in brackets should be cut out:

(a distance of) ten yards
(advance) planning – who goes in for retrospective planning?
(advance) warning – a warning wouldn't be much good if it weren't in advance
(at a) later (date)
at some time (to come)
(awkward) predicament – you can't have an easy predicament
came (at a time) when
commute (back and forth)
(complete) monopoly – a monopoly has to be complete, total
consensus (of opinion)
(difficult) dilemma
during (the course of)
equal (to one another)
estimated (roughly at)
filled (to capacity)
for (a period of) six months
(foreign) imports
(hot) water heater
indicted (on a charge)
introduced (for the first time)
look back (in retrospect)
(major) breakthrough
never (at any time)
(originally) created
(partially) destroyed – if it were so, it would be damaged
postponed (until later)
reported (to the effect that)
(rough) rule of thumb

since (the time when)
(suddenly) exploded – a slow explosion would be interesting
(underground) subway
(unexpected) surprise
(unintentional) mistake – as opposed to all those intentional
mistakes........

Think about the precise meaning of the words you're using and don't
embellish them unnecessarily. You're not writing to fill a newspaper, nor
to reach a count of 500 words for an essay at school (when some of the
above phrases came in very useful). Cut, cut cut!

And while we're on the subject of cutting, here are some more candidates:

in order to – leave out 'in order'; the little word 'to' already
has a sense of purpose: 'We need to meet in order to finalise
the budget'/'We need to meet to finalise the budget'

for the purpose of – 'for' or 'to' will suffice

it is apparent/obvious/evident/clear that – always a dodgy
thing to write; it may be apparent to you but not necessarily
to your reader, and what does it add? 'It is apparent that
problems exist in the finance department'/'Problems exist
in the finance department' – is there a difference?

it would be greatly appreciated if – usually
you can substitute 'please ....'

it should be noted that – if you're writing clearly, you shouldn't
have to resort to those irritating little messages to the reader

Nine

Building rapport
with the reader

This section is to do with tone, emotion, the feeling behind the words and the feeling generated in the reader. It's easier to get this right if you know your readers but even then it's possible for your message to misfire; if you don't know your readers, you have to make an inspired guess at what will work.

In chapter 6, we discussed George Orwell's rules. Number 5 was 'avoid stock phrases'. When I was a student in the sixties, I did secretarial work to earn money. This was the time of typewriters, carbon copy paper, typewriter rubbers and tippex; making a mistake involved labour-intensive action to delete the mistake, or a fresh start. The language of the correspondence was quite unlike that used by normal people; in fact people referred to it as 'commercial' or 'business' language.

Letters would start with:

With reference to your correspondence dated the 14th inst. (an abbreviation of 'instant' meaning the current month) which was received in this office on the 16th inst.........

or

I am in receipt of your missive post-marked the 20th of this month.....

And they would end with:

I beg to remain your obedient servant..... (if only!)

or

Rest assured of our best attention at all times (particularly irritating if the reason for contacting them was to complain when there had obviously been a blip in the 'best attention')

or

Please do not hesitate to make contact with this office should you have any further queries.

My theory about why this language persisted for so long is simply that it was habit and custom. Before email, a copy of each letter sent would be kept on file; when asked to write a letter, the logical starting point would be to refer to the file. If you were new to the office, you certainly didn't question the strange language that peppered the pages in the file – you just copied it, assuming that that was the preferred style. And so it would have gone on for decades.

There's nothing grammatically wrong with those phrases but the advent of email and its widespread use has introduced a much less formal style of language. One of the main reasons for this is that secretaries have more or less disappeared. Up to the end of the sixties, no man would voluntarily refer to himself as a typist. The arrival of computers changed all that: 'keyboard operator' is quite a different story. Now, everyone is at it, and mostly those are self-taught typists without the discipline of secretarial training or pre-conceived ideas of 'correct' language. It's the reason for this book!

Most commercial organisations these days strive to communicate with us at almost a social level – and that can misfire if we think it's inappropriately friendly. I don't wish to be addressed as 'Dear Madam' but I take exception to being addressed as 'Dear Jenifer' by someone with whom I've had no previous contact. But that's me, and perhaps my age group.

We don't generally use the stock phrases mentioned above because they sound pompous and old-fashioned but other ones have taken their place – and I still notice the last one creeping in as an easy sign-off:

Please don't hesitate to contact me if you have any queries.

In an era when most people are attached to their mobile phones with an umbilical cord, is it likely that they'd hesitate? And we're no longer in awe of the professions or commercial organisations; we'd have no hesitation whatsoever in ringing them up and giving them an earful.

The sign-off is like a parting handshake and it needs to be relevant to the communication and to sound sincere:

- I hope this information helps. Give me a call if you have any questions.
- Please use my direct line number if you'd like to discuss this.
- Please let me know if you'd like us to go ahead with this.

- I need your agreement to this by 14 April if we are to meet the deadline.
- If I don't hear from you by 14 April, I'll assume you don't want us to pursue this option.
- Thanks again for bringing this to my attention.

Or nothing. If you're writing to a colleague and you've given the information asked of you, why not leave it at that?

What about the starters? There's a difference between responding to a letter and an email. When replying to an email, most of us press the reply button so the instigator of the communication is up to speed with the request. There's no need for any preamble; you can get straight into the response.

With a letter, you probably need to remind the reader why you're writing:

- You've asked for information about the XYZ machine
- Thanks for your letter of 14 May
- I was sorry/disappointed to receive your letter complaining about our service
- Many thanks for inviting me to your reception on ......
- I was delighted to hear the news that you had ....
- You've asked for my views on the latest events at head office

And you should always use a heading; it gives the reader instant information.

If you're starting the email communication, rather than responding, get straight to the point, as we discussed under structure in chapter 3.

I have a meeting on 12 March with XYZ company and need some information about the ABC project.

Then you can expand on what you need and why, and the reader will read it knowing the context.

The message here is: know your audience, or at least have the will and the imagination to try and make sure your communication hits the target. Put yourself in your reader's shoes. Initially it might take some effort to wean yourself off your own stock phrases but it's worth the effort. Even if you have devised some wonderfully sincere-sounding sign-off, if you use it all the time, its sincerity quotient will rapidly reduce.

The same applies to spoken phrases in their ability to irritate. I once had to make a series of phone calls to a client. The first time, he responded to my call by saying: "Jen!! How the devil are you?" It sounded flatteringly enthusiastic and interested. I was quite bowled over ......The second time, he said the very same thing. And the third, and its effect rapidly became negative.

Stick your head above the parapet This is a very important point. If you want to influence people at work and gain their respect, commit yourself in writing. Never write 'I will try ....' Look at the difference:

1. I will have the figures with you by noon on Tuesday.
2. I will try and have the figures with you by noon on Tuesday.

The first promotes confidence in the reader: Hooray! The figures will be with me on Tuesday. The second is decidedly iffy; the underlying message is 'well, at the moment maybe I'll be able to get the figures to you by Tuesday but if something more important comes along – and frankly your figures aren't really that important to me – I'll do that first and you'll just have to wait.'

It's not good enough. It's not good enough for customers and it's not good enough for colleagues. As a mantra for success at work, 'under-promise and over-deliver' is hard to beat. Customers love commitment: "We'll have the spare part with you by Friday" – and it arrives on Thursday. Wow! And it even works if, on Tuesday, you have to get back in touch with customer and say: "I'm so sorry – we can't get it to you until Monday." At least they know.

And colleagues would love commitment if it were ever shown to them. Imagine the transformation at work if everyone actually cooperated, agreed to deadlines and met them. The reduction in stress and frustration would be palpable. How can you plan without knowing the deadlines? How do you prioritise? I'm not suggesting you dig yourself into a hole by making wild commitments you have no hope of meeting. Just be honest with people but commit yourself, and do your utmost to meet the commitment – and keep them updated if you're going to let them down, and grovel.

It's the power of positive writing.

Finally, the great advantage of writing is that it's not spontaneous. You can look at it again the next morning before sending it – always a good idea if the subject is difficult or contentious. You can check it out with colleagues and seek their opinions if it's really important. It's sometimes difficult to assess the likely effect your written words will have; you've written them and heard them in a certain way which won't necessarily be shared by your readers. Take the time to try and reduce any negative effects.

Ten

Exploiting email:
the etiquette

Email is a fantastic piece of technology and enables us to communicate
with lightning speed. But we need to use it thoughtfully to get the
best out of it; if we don't, it clogs up the channels of communication,
makes us inefficient and wastes money.

The use of email in the work place is seductive. It's clear evidence
that you're doing something and you can copy other people in on the
communication so they know you're doing something too. For conveying
straight bits of information, it's rather better than the phone; you don't
need to get involved in a dialogue, or to phone four people with the same
message.

But how often do you observe, or get involved in yourself, a series of
emails going to and fro, eating up people's time, when one phone call
would have sorted it all out? And if you work in an organisation where
paranoia reigns and written evidence is a must, why not have the phone
call to sort it all out and then confirm the result and future action by
email?

Email can be extremely efficient if used in the right way; used in the wrong way, it can be disastrous. Why do you think some companies have banned the use of email one day a week? It's because they suspect its use is an energy sink, hinders internal communication and stops people getting on with what they're really meant to be doing.

People allow email to dominate; it's a sort of tyranny. If you work in a set-up where your job is to respond to emails 100% of the time, you just have to get on with it. But most people have a variety of activities to do, one of which will be to respond to emails. Why do we expect a same-hour or even same-day response? It's arrogant and unreasonable and, most of the time, quite unnecessary. If you have a seriously urgent request, a phone call would be a better option.

This knee-jerk reaction to emails makes people and organisations less efficient for three reasons.

- If you leave your email facility on, and allow it to beep at you every time a new email arrives, you allow yourself to be constantly interrupted; this ruins concentration and will probably increase your stress level.

- If you decide to read the email..........."Oh hell, that's John, I wonder what he wants..." and if your brain has embarked on this route, you may as well read it because it's already a distraction, you allow yourself to get sucked into what may be a trivial activity.

- If you then decide to respond to the email, you're diverting your attention from what you were doing – which presumably was important – to something which could probably wait until you'd finished the important activity.

Our effectiveness is a function of our ability to concentrate; as we discussed in section three, we can only concentrate on one thing at a time. So we have a duty to ourselves and our employers to do our utmost to create conditions that will enable us to concentrate. It's your decision. I have no sympathy for people who wail about the vast number of emails they receive, who work so terribly hard, arrive early, stay late but never seem to get the important things done, never quite meet the deadlines.

- Switch off email!
- Introduce a discipline of looking at it, say, 3 times a day.
- Decide what the important activities are and don't get diverted.

And managers and team leaders beware. Don't conspire with email to make your team members inefficient. Don't be guilty of sending emails to them and expecting an immediate response. Prima donnas at work are a pain.

This is a book about writing, not about time management. So here are some guidelines to help you use email more effectively and save time for you and your colleagues, customers and suppliers.

Please don't . . . .

- use all capitalised letters – it's known as SHOUTING
- copy people unless it's essential
- forward a message that's been forwarded to you; open the original and forward that one
- forward messages without explaining why you've done so
- use email to avoid personal contact; if it's a delicate or difficult situation, phone or see them face to face

- print incoming messages unless absolutely necessary; it wastes time, paper and money
- clog up the system by sending trivial messages
- pass on any chain-mail type messages, no matter how hilarious or heart-rending
- expect an immediate response; if it's really urgent, use the phone
- impose unreasonable demands on your recipients
- send sensitive information by email – it might end up in the wrong hands, you might end up in court or you might lose your job (remember the email trails used in the Leveson inquiry, the fate of Damian Green, the famous phrase: 'it's a good day to bury bad news....')
- leave your email switched on so it interrupts you like the phone; the good thing about it is that you can decide when to deal with new messages
- ask for receipts unless absolutely necessary
- blind copy people, definitely not the recipient's manager – you'll make enemies

Please do ....

- consider if email is the best way to get your message across; it may be easiest for you but not easiest for the person receiving it
- plan what you want to write before hitting the keyboard, and think about logic and structure
- use a subject heading
- keep your message brief; try to keep it to one screen
- use helpful headings within the text
- make it easy for the reader; layout, punctuation, spelling and grammar still matter, particularly when it's going external

- be considerate about what you attach; fun photos, colour and groovy graphics may look good but they take an age to download
- tell people who send you unwanted messages to remove your name from the list
- check your mailbox at least once a day, or make sure you use the automatic response facility so the sender knows when you're likely to read the message

Eleven

Writing for an international audience

Our laziness for learning languages is boosted by the fact that English has become the international language of business and technology. It had a head start with the imperial legacy when the use of English became widespread across our colonies and is, of course, reinforced by its use in America. We have to thank our lucky stars that the Americans didn't opt for German – apparently it was a close shave.

Now that's a good example: 'a close shave'. I'm writing this book for people with a working use of English and I'd be delighted if foreigners working in English also read it. I'm trying to speak to you, the reader, so am making the text as colloquial as possible. But if I were being really considerate to an audience with English as their second – or third – language, I would use a different expression.

The fact that so few British people speak other languages makes them insensitive to the nuances of language. English-speaking foreigners find it easier to understand the English spoken by other foreigners who are unlikely to indulge in idiomatic language. We live and work in a globalised world. If we want to communicate, we have to be aware of sliding into language that's ambiguous or confusing, even with Americans: to quote George Bernard Shaw, 'England and America are two countries divided by a common language'.

People learning English avoid using what we call phrasal verbs. Expressions like 'let down' or 'brush up on' are a real problem even for speakers of languages such as Dutch that have similar constructions. So their use will probably cause confusion in both speech and writing.

Let's take the verb 'to put' as an example. It normally means 'to place' as in 'I **put** the book on the table'. Then we add the word 'up' as in 'I **put up** the picture in the hallway' but it can also mean 'to give someone accommodation' as in 'Please will you **put up** my son this weekend'. Then we add another word, 'with', and '**put up with**' means something quite different, 'to tolerate' as in 'I'm not prepared to **put up with** this behaviour'. It's not easy, but it is easy – with a bit of consideration – to avoid using words or phrases where the reader could misinterpret the meaning.

Let's look more closely at the word 'up'. This two-letter word has more meanings than any other two-letter word; it can be used as five different parts of speech: an adverb, adjective, preposition, noun and verb – see the next section for an explanation of parts of speech.

It's easy to understand **up**, meaning toward the sky or at the top of the list, but when we awaken in the morning, why do we wake **up**?

At a meeting, why does a topic come **up**? Why do we speak **up**, and why are the officers **up** for election (if there's a tie, it's a toss **up**) and why is it **up** to the secretary to write **up** a report? We call **up** our friends, brighten

up a room, polish **up** the silver, warm **up** the leftovers and clean **up** the kitchen. We lock **up** the house and fix **up** the old car.

At other times, this little word has special meaning. People stir **up** trouble, line **up** for tickets, work **up** an appetite, and think **up** excuses. To be dressed is one thing but to be dressed **up** is special.

And this **up** is confusing: a drain must be opened **up** because it is blocked **up.**

We open **up** a store in the morning but we close it **up** at night. We seem to be pretty mixed **up** about **up**!

To be knowledgeable about the proper uses of **up**, look it **up** in the dictionary. In a desk-sized dictionary, it takes **up** almost 1/4 of the page and can add **up** to about thirty definitions.

If you're **up** to it, you might try building **up** a list of the many ways we use **up**. It will take **up** a lot of your time, but if you don't give **up**, you may wind **up** with **up** to a hundred or more.

When it threatens to rain, we say it's clouding **up**. When the sun comes out, we say it's clearing **up**. When it rains, the earth soaks it **up**; when it doesn't rain for a while, things dry **up**. One could go on and on, but I'll wrap it **up** for now – my time is **up**.

Non native English speakers are increasingly part of our national workforce so we need to take that into account when writing internally as well as when communicating internationally. It requires a sensitivity to the fact that our wonderful language contains many words – spelt exactly the same way – that have quite different meanings depending on the context. As a native English speaker, you don't even question it; the meaning will be obvious. For example:

This account is **outstanding**. For someone working in the accounts department, the meaning is obvious. But for anyone else who understands 'outstanding' to mean 'conspicuous, eminent, excellent' it sounds rather odd. Why not be safe and use 'unpaid'?

Right has at least 25 meanings without even venturing into rap lingo, including:

Turn right – direction
That's right – correct, or morally just
Right! Let's go – exclamation
The engine doesn't sound right – in a normal condition
He's to the right of his party – favouring conservatism
I have the right to do this – a moral permit
I am right handed – as opposed to left handed
We have to right the wrong that has been done to us –
perhaps a little outmoded but it means to sort out, avenge;
you can also 'right' a boat that has capsized
Do it right now – immediately

And so it goes on – the Oxford English dictionary has a whole column devoted to how we use the word 'right' including the idiom 'as right as rain' – meaning perfectly sound, in good health.

So use your words with care. Be aware of the potential for ambiguity. It's important in both speech and writing but when you're speaking, you can usually see if your listeners don't understand, and they can always ask you to clarify. Your readers are on their own, trying to work out what you mean. Again, we're not talking about dumbing down. Just think about your audience and express yourself as simply as possible without resorting to idioms or jargon.

Part three: The technical bits

12. Getting the grammar right

Parts of speech, the basics, ten common
errors and how to avoid them

13. Words which cause confusion

Look-alike words with different meanings

14. Punctuation

Why it's so important, definitions, when to use it

15. Spelling

The rules - we were never taught them at school but they exist

16. Checklist for writing and editing

Twelve

Getting the grammar right

Our lack of linguistic skills as a nation has another disadvantage: one of the benefits of learning foreign languages is the insight it gives us into the make-up and structure of our own language. Those of you who went to school at any time since the seventies probably won't have had the pleasure of learning grammar. This doesn't help you write correctly or with confidence. Grammar is the rules governing our language. We need those rules in the same way that a game of football needs rules.

I was shocked to hear a speaker on Radio 4 put forward the theory that there should be no such thing as a mistake in the use of the English language. He claimed to consider it acceptable for someone to say: 'most beautifulest'. Agreed, I would understand what the speaker was trying to say, but my impression would be of someone who is verging on the illiterate. Why condemn people to the abyss of ignorance?

We associate an ability to write clearly and correctly with an ability to think. People who can't spell or express themselves clearly will struggle to be successful. It's worth investing a bit of time to understand the basics of our language. Grammar-check can help; I always leave it switched on just in case but you can't rely on it.

This is where we need to make the distinction between writing and speaking. Dialects add colour and interest to our nation; slang is fun and 15-year olds tend to speak rather differently from 50-year olds. Frequently people speak ungrammatically to suit the image they want to project. "Me and Harry are going skateboarding" isn't correct but my nephew from north London simply wouldn't accept saying: "Harry and I are going skateboarding". He gets away with it in speech, to his mates, but not in writing. But people who always speak ungrammatically certainly have more difficulty writing correctly if they don't understand the grammar.

In many ways, our language is delightfully uncomplicated despite the examples given in section 11. For instance, we have one word 'the' which stays the same regardless of which noun it is attached to and whether that noun is being used as the subject or object of the sentence. In German, there are three classes of nouns – masculine, feminine and neuter – and the 'the' word is der, die or das depending on the 'gender' of the noun. Not only does that change depending on how you're using the noun, the noun itself has different endings depending on how it is 'declined' – that's the grammatical term. But you don't have to know that to learn English, so take heart.

This isn't going to be a lengthy explanation of English grammar; I'm just going to cover:

- what I consider to be the absolute minimum that you need to know to be able to write correctly with confidence
- the most common mistakes and how to avoid them

Parts of speech The dictionary definition of a part of speech is: 'each of the categories to which words are assigned in accordance with their grammatical and semantic functions'.

Being able to identify parts of speech enables us to know what the word is doing in the sentence; it matters because some words change their spelling depending on how you're using them. It also enables us to put together sentences which make sense. One word may be several different parts of speech; its position in the sentence will indicate how you're using it. There are conventions in every language for the order of words; it's called syntax.

There are eight main parts of speech, italicised in the examples below.

Nouns are naming words: **proper** nouns are names and start with a capital letter, **common** nouns don't. Nouns tend to be the guts of the sentence, they give us vital information.

When *Janet* lived in *France* she had to rely on a *well* in her *garden* for all her *water*.

'Janet' and 'France' are proper nouns so start with a capital letter. Nouns are the key words. In speech, with a bit of imaginative sign language, you could probably work out the meaning of the sentence with just the nouns; you wouldn't have a clue without them. If you were doing a mind map, you would tend to use nouns.

Pronouns take the place of nouns; they're substitutes and avoid having to constantly repeat the nouns which would be very tedious.

Jean Thomas is married to Greg Smith. When *she* first met *him she* was working as a personal assistant at the Department of the Environment.

Pronouns can cause us some problems because some of them change depending on whether we're using them as the subject or object of the sentence. More of that later.

Adjectives describe nouns; they help us to picture the scene, adding colour and interest.

Jim planned his *new* identity. He dyed his hair *blond*, grew a *short* beard and bought a pair of *rimless* glasses.

That sentence would be far less interesting and informative if it were:

Jim planned his identity. He dyed his hair, grew a beard and bought a pair of glasses.

Verbs: the 'doing' or 'being' words; they tell us what's happening, the activity, and when it happened, the tense – whether it's past, present or future. The nouns and the verbs convey the main message in any sentence.

Jim *planned* his new identity. He *dyed* his hair blond, *grew* a short beard and *bought* a pair of rimless glasses.

Verbs can cause some problems because most of them change depending on tense and conjugation. For example, we write: 'I *was* at home last night' but 'We *were* at home last night'. 'He *was* with me but they *were* at the theatre'.

Adverbs: describe how the verb is being done – 'ad' 'verb', it's easy when you get the hang of it. Like adjectives, they give you a verbal paint brush to create a picture for your readers. 80% of them end in **ly** so they're easy to spot.

John walked *quickly* down the alley. He was breathing *heavily*. *Foolishly*, he decided to stop and look behind him.

Those three short sentences would lose their dramatic tension without the adverbs.

John walked down the alley. He was breathing. He decided to stop and look behind him.

Conjunctions are joining words; they join phrases or short sentences so the pace of writing isn't too staccato and abrupt.

I went to the storeroom *and* looked for the file, *but* there was no sign of it.

It would sound a bit robotic to write:

I went to the storeroom. I looked for the file. There was no sign of it.

The most common conjunctions are **and**, **but** and **because**. I remember my teachers saying, in the early sixties, that you should never start a sentence with and, but or because, because they are conjunctions and their function is to join words or phrases. But that was then. You'll notice that journalists and other writers break the rule and you can do so too if you're trying to make a point. But don't overdo it.

Prepositions tell you the position of something, or the relationship between things; they are those little words like in, on, over, under, with, above, below, to.

I realised there was another cupboard *behind* the door. *Above* this cupboard were two boxes.

Two things to remember about prepositions:

- After a preposition, you should use the object form of the word; this only matters when you're using pronouns where the form changes. 'Please give the money to Michael or I' is incorrect; it should be 'Please give the money to Michael or me.' Don't despair – there's more about this later.

- Try to avoid ending a sentence with a preposition. This is where the difference between writing and speaking really kicks in. People will often say something like: "Who did you give it to?" Correctly, it should be "To whom did you give it?" but in speech you'd sound as if you had a plum rammed down your throat if you used the correct syntax. There's also a problem with our phrasal verbs which have a distinct meaning. In section 11 we had the example of 'put up with' meaning 'to tolerate'. Winston Churchill was reprimanded by a civil servant for ending a sentence with a preposition and famously responded by writing: 'This is one rule up with which I will not put.'

Interjections are exclamations, something that interrupts the flow of the sentence, when you are exclaiming!

> *Help!* I can't carry this table.
> *Oh,* must we?
> *Right!* Let's get going.

They're used far more often in speech than in writing but the informal nature of email allows them to creep in. Use with caution in business writing (see section 14 on Punctuation).

So those are the eight parts of speech. In addition we have two 'articles' which we use in front of nouns or their adjectives:

the definite article: **the** – the man in the car = a specific, definite man in a specific, definite car
the indefinite article: **a** – a man in a car = any man in any car
and it's **an** in front of a word beginning with a vowel, a, e, i, o, u:
an advantage, an elephant, an idea, an obstacle, an urgent need.

The other two words you need to know about are **subject** and **object**. A sentence needs to have a subject – a noun or pronoun – that the sentence is about and with which the verb needs to **agree**; in English the form of the verb sometimes changes depending on the subject, whether it is singular or plural. A sentence must also have a verb, to tell us what the subject is doing, and it will usually have an **object**; the noun or pronoun that is on the receiving end of the activity of the verb. Examples:

The English love dogs.
Subject   verb   object

Children enjoy playing on the beach
subject   verb   object

I mentioned 'syntax' above. The dictionary describes it as 'the grammatical arrangement of words showing their connection and relation'. I like to think of it as a convention, a code, a shared way of expressing ourselves that helps us communicate. Imagine life without syntax. That previous sentence would be all jumbled up and you'd struggle to work out the meaning:

Helps think a code way a shared expressing convention like of I as a it ourselves that communicate to us of

Syntax changes for different languages. In English we make it as simple as possible. An adjective will usually come before the noun it's describing. An adverb usually comes after the verb. We start with the subject and include the verb as soon as possible so the reader knows what's happening. In German, the verb comes right at the end of the sentence, so that sentence would be:

In German, the verb right at the end of the sentence comes.

With English as our mother tongue, we learn about syntax from a very early age – even though we don't know what it's called. Most people will naturally speak with the right syntax; we just have to write it right as well.

Ten tangles with grammar

I've narrowed this down to the ten most frequent errors I come across in the hope that, by explaining them, you'll know how to avoid making them.

1. Pronouns

The problem with pronouns is that there are four different types, each of which has a specific use. Also, unlike nouns, they can change depending on whether they are the **subject** or **object** of the sentence. Here they are:

subject	object	reflexive	possessive
I	me	myself	my/mine
he	him	himself	his

she	her	herself	her/s
it	it	itself	its
we	us	ourselves	our/s
you	you	yourself/ves	your/s
they	them	themselves	their/s
who	whom		whose
(one	one	oneself	one's)

So many people, particularly songwriters and politicians, use pronouns incorrectly that you may be tempted to give up. Please don't, as the rules are straightforward:

- when the pronoun is the subject of the sentence, you use the subject form
- when it is the object, or **when it follows a preposition**, use the object form

I took my coat to the dry cleaners.
John and I went to the cinema last night.
John came with me to the dry cleaners and then we had a coffee.
John and I were having coffee when you interrupted us.
You gave the message to us and then John left with you. I stayed behind.

Reflexive pronouns
The main culprit is **myself** (hotly followed by **ourselves**). Its incorrect use has mushroomed over the last few years as either:

- a substitute for **me**, on the grounds that it's more polite – when it's just wrong

- a substitute for **I**, presumably when the writer or speaker can't remember whether they should use I or me and goes for myself as the soft option, as in 'Myself and Anne attended the conference last week' (**ouch!**). It should be 'Anne and I attended the conference last week'.

Its correct use is this: when it reflects back to its own subject form. Draw horizontal lines joining the lists above; you can only use the reflexive pronoun that is on the same line, owned, by the subject pronoun, or noun, as in:

I hit **myself** with the hammer.
You must do it **yourself**.
He'll hurt **himself** if he doesn't stop that.
She threw **herself** onto the sofa and burst into tears.
Harry hurt **himself** while skateboarding.
We always have to do it **ourselves**.
The cat licked **itself** all over.
They worked it all out **themselves**.

Possessive pronouns
Each pronoun has its own possessive version, as above, so you just have to use the right one.

I carried **my** bag. This bag is **mine**.
He gave all **his** money to charity.
Please move **your** car from **my** space.
Our hope is to succeed.
Whose is this book?
Their quality of work was terrible.
The dog wagged **its** tail.

Notice that the possessive pronoun **its** doesn't need an apostrophe – see below. The only time you use an apostrophe with 'its' is when it's the abbreviated form of 'it is' – 'it's'. If you're tempted to whack in an apostrophe, ask yourself if you could substitute 'it is'.

2. The apostrophe

English is the only language that uses an apostrophe in the ways we use it. It causes such confusion that there have been calls for its abolition. That would be a great shame because it's a useful little thing and it has two precise uses.

To show that you've missed out a letter, or letters, in abbreviated words. For example:

- We'll see you tonight.
- John's late again.
- It's way past midnight.

To indicate possession or ownership. This means you can shorten the text and avoid putting 'of the' or 'belonging to'. For example:

- Let me see John's laptop (the laptop belonging to John)
- The children's toys are all over the place (the toys of the children)
- The director's report makes interesting reading (the report of the director)

In the examples above, John, children and director are all nouns and they own, respectively, the laptop, toys and report. So the 's has to be attached to the nouns.

If the noun is plural, for example, 'directors', you indicate this by putting the apostrophe after the s. Effectively you're writing 'The directors's report makes interesting reading' but because there's already an 's' with the plural of 'directors' you miss off the second 's' – so it should be

- The directors' report makes interesting reading (the report of several directors)

You need the apostrophe to indicate that special meaning of ownership, 'of the'; without it, the word would simply be plural, lots of directors. So it follows that you NEVER use 's to make a noun plural – greengrocers and signwriters take note. Most nouns take either an 's', 'es' or 'ies' to become plural. Some don't, like men, women and children. And some nouns can be singular or plural, like fish, fruit and sheep. But most of them become plural by adding 's' or 'es' so if you're indicating ownership, you just add the apostrophe after the final 's'.

Horses' hooves are dangerous.
Cars' tyres must be checked at the MoT.
The chairs' height must be matched to the table.
The girls' skirts were a little too short for the chilly weather.

(There's a test at the end.)

3. Sentences

A sentence has to make sense; to do that, it needs a verb, and that form of the verb needs to be what is called **finite** – finished off.

'Following your letter of 8 April.' This is wrong because it isn't a sentence – it has no finite verb; there is no action.

There are three forms of the verb that aren't finite and they are called:

the infinitive	to write
the present participle	writing
the past participle	written

These groups of words are not sentences:

- black pen to complete the form
- writing out your name in full
- anything not written in blue or black ink

They need a finite form of the verb to make sense, so:

You should use a black or blue pen to complete the form.
Writing out your name in full **is essential**.
Anything not written in blue or black ink **will be ignored**.

4. Subject and verb agreement

Nouns and verbs are the most important parts of speech as they give us hard facts. The verb tells us what's going on and when. The form of the verb changes depending on:

- **tense** – past, present, future ....and there are others but let's keep it simple

- **person** - there are three of them:
  the first person refers to 'I' and 'we'
  the second person refers to 'you' which stays
  as 'you' whether it's one or more people
  the third person refers to 'he',' she', 'it', 'they'

- whether the person is singular or plural. In grammar-speak, this is the verb **_agreeing_** with its subject. People often get this wrong in speech:

We **was** halfway across the room before we saw her. (should be **were**)
I **were** the last person to leave. (should be **was**)
There **is** many people I need to see. (should be **are**)

We may get away with grammatical mistakes when we speak but we don't when we write.

5. Linking sentences with commas

One of the few strict rules about punctuation (see next section) is that you can't link sentences with commas. So 'I walked round the corner, I was just in time to see him go.' has to be:

I walked round the corner. I was just in
time to see him go. (full stop)
I walked round the corner; I was just in
time to see him go. (semi colon)
I walked round the corner and I was just in
time to see him go. (conjunction)

6. Splitting the infinitive

Splitting the infinitive is a fault that can only happen in English because the infinitive consists of two words: 'to' and the stem of the verb – 'to polish' for example. In French, the infinitive of 'to polish' is 'cirer', one word only.

So, in English you could put:

He failed to completely polish the car. Here the infinitive is split by putting 'completely' between 'to' and 'polish'. It would be more correct as:

He failed to polish the car completely.

But make sure you don't alter the meaning

He completely failed to polish the car means he hasn't polished the car at all. The same words used in a different order will change the meaning.

In some people's eyes, splitting the infinitive should be a crime punishable by death, but let's be reasonable. Try to avoid splitting the infinitive but *To boldly go* .... is a famous example of a writer who didn't care about this rule. If there's a creative reason for doing it, you can get away with it but, as a general rule, try to avoid it.

7. Anyone someone no one

They have **one** in them so they always need the singular form of the verb and shouldn't be followed later by **they** or **their**. If you want to avoid the clumsy he/she, his/her by using they, start off with a plural:

- *Anyone wanting to go to Italy this summer must put their name on the list* is plain wrong.
- *Anyone wanting to go to Italy this summer must put his/her name on the list* is clumsy, and would be much more digestible as
- *All those wanting to go to Italy this summer must put their names on the list.*

or, easier still, use **you**

- *If you want to go to Italy this summer, put your name on the list.*

8. Each

Think of 'each' as a shortened version of 'every one of'. As such, it must always be followed by a singular form of the verb:

Each of our shops is well supplied. (Each is the true subject of the sentence; **of our shops** is simply describing **each**.)

9. Collective nouns

These are singular nouns that refer to groups: team, government, board, herd, school. Being singular, they should be followed by a singular verb:

The herd of cattle was a good buy.

But there is some flexibility.

- If they are one unit, then the noun is best treated as singular: *The cabinet has decided against hanging.*
- If they are being thought of as individuals, then the collective noun is best treated as plural: *The cabinet have decided to support free TV licences for pensioners.*

The main thing is not to change your mind halfway through a sentence:

*The government has decided **they** want to raise taxes* is wrong, and should be *The government has decided **it wants** to raise taxes.*

10. Pernickety but important

- **Less/fewer, number of/amount of**

I refuse to accept that this little rule should be abandoned despite the fact that even presenters on Radio 4 sometimes get it wrong. The principle is simple:

If you can count it, use 'fewer' or 'number of'. If you can't count it, use 'less' or 'amount of'.

fewer cars	less traffic
number of cars	amount of traffic
fewer bottles of wine	less wine
number of bottles of wine	amount of wine (or 'volume' might be better as wine is a liquid)

- **Different from** and **different to**

The only time you should use 'different to' is when you're writing 'That looks different to me'. If you're differentiating one thing from another, it should be 'different from', as in: 'This book has different recipes from those on the website.'

- **Compare with** and **compare to**

Use 'compare with' if you're describing differences. For example: 'If we compare France with England, the populations are about the same but France is twice as big.'

Use 'compare to' if you're likening two things. For example: 'She was frequently compared to Marilyn Munroe.'

- **Between**

The word has the notion of two-ness within it so you can only use it with two units. For example, 'The proceeds from the house were split between him and his brother.'

If there are more than two units, you have to use 'among'. 'The proceeds of the house were divided among the four children.'

- **Where/were/we're**

This is here only because I sometimes see confusion about their use because they sound similar. And there's no rule to help you. My only suggestion is to think about the meaning of the word.

- 'Where' is to do with place and is made up of 'w' and 'here', also to do with place. **Where** did you put the file?
- 'Were' is the past participle of the verb 'to be': They **were** standing in the rain.
- 'We're' is the abbreviated version of 'we are': **We're** delighted you can join us on Friday at the team meeting. If you can't substitute 'we are' for 'we're', don't use it.

- **There/their/they're**

Similar confusion exists with these three. Similar solutions:

- 'There' is to do with place, 't' + 'here'. Don't just stand there, come in. Try and avoid starting a sentence with 'There are .....' as in 'There are many problems involved in getting funding for this project'. It's woolly writing; much better to write: 'Many problems exist in getting funding for this project.'
- 'Their' is the possessive pronoun belonging to 'they': They took their files and left the meeting.
- 'They're' is the abbreviated version of 'they are': They're always late by at least fifteen minutes. If you can't substitute 'they are' for 'they're', don't use it.

- **Who/whom/whose**

  - 'Who' refers to people and it is a pronoun. We should say 'Who will be at the meeting?' not 'Which people will be at the meeting?' It's the subject form of the word. Similarly, it should be 'The residents who fetched the sandbags.....' 'The residents that or which fetched the sandbags' is wrong.
  - 'Whom' is the object form; it's falling out of practice in speech and very informal writing but it certainly hasn't disappeared. You use it when you need to use the object form, as in: 'The manager, whom I saw making a phone call in the corridor, should have been at the meeting.' The main sentence is 'The manager should have been at the meeting'; the subsidiary sentence is: 'I saw him making a phone call'. 'I' is still the subject of that clause when you combine the two. If the sentence had been 'The manager who made a phone call in the corridor should have been at the meeting.' you use 'who' because it is the

subject of the clause as well as the sentence; if it was a separate sentence, it would be 'He made a phone call in the corridor.'

- 'Whose' can be used as a pronoun – of or belonging to which person: 'Whose is this file?' It can also be used as an adjective: 'The man, whose name was John ....' Not to be confused with 'who's' which sounds exactly the same but means 'who is': 'Who's coming to the cinema this evening?'

Thirteen

Words which cause confusion

Y ou need to be aware of parts of speech – see Grammar section – to understand this, particularly the jobs of nouns, adjectives and verbs.

Where I've emboldened a letter, I'm suggesting it'll help you remember what's what. And I'm defining the words as they're generally used, not giving you a dictionary.

accept	receive, welcome, give an affirmative answer
except	not including
access	the way in, entrance
excess	too much
advice	helpful comment – it's a noun
advise	to give a helpful comment – it's a verb. Remember, the words with a **c** at the end are nouns and the ones with **s** at the end are verbs. The same rule applies to practice (noun) and practise (verb), licence (noun) and license (verb), device (noun) and devise (verb). Spellcheck will never pick this up.

affect   to be **a**ltered in some way (he was affected by his long illness) – verb

effect   result – when used as a noun (the effect will be disastrous). Can also be a verb, meaning to have an end result (We must effect change to be successful.) But usually, affect is used as a verb and effect is used as a noun.

prescribe   impose authoritatively, or advise the use of

proscribe   banish, exile, reject

aural   to do with ears and hearing

oral   to do with mouths and speaking

canvass   seek (as in canvass opinion) – verb

canvas   thick material – noun

stationary   standing still (think of c**ar**s on the M25)

stationery   office paper and pens (**e** is for envelopes)

elicit   to draw out (elicit information)

illicit   illegal (as in illicit drugs)

eligible   available

legible   read-able

foreword   text at the beginning of a book or chapter

forward   onward, towards the front

lose   cease to have – it's a verb (I always lose when I gamble)

loose   not confined or tethered – it's an adjective (She was a loose woman)

principal	the head of a school or college (**a l**eader) – used as a noun, or m**a**in – when used as an adjective (the princip**a**l street)
principle	a ru**le** or **e**thic – always a noun (The principle of life ....)
allude	refer to
elude	avoid
collaborate	work with
corroborate	support (as in corroborating evidence)
complement	the whole (comes from the verb 'to complete') when used as a noun; to complement – verb – means to make complete (eg The team members complemented each other – means all their skills worked well together. It doesn't mean they were constantly admiring each other's hairstyles!)
compliment	a word of pra**i**se – a noun. **I** like getting compl**i**ments.
concise	short, succinct
precise	accurate
cite	to quote - verb
site	a place – noun, or to place – verb
sight	vision - noun
dependant	the person who depends
dependent	the state of depending
council	body of people, as in town council
counsel	advice, often legal – noun, or to advise – verb (counsellor comes from it: marriage guidance, crisis, victim support)

currant	dried fruit
current	existing – adjective, or the flow in water – noun
draft	rough copy
draught	current of air coming through a window, a measure of liquor
lead	to be at the head of – verb (pronounced **lee**d). Not to be confused with lead – noun (pronounced **le**d) – a heavy metal
led	the past participle of the verb 'to lead' (He led the team onto the pitch)
eminent	very important
imminent	about to happen
discreet	subtle, sensitive, diplomatic (He made discreet enquiries)
discrete	separate from, distinct (Business development is a discrete function within the organisation.)
enquiry	a question seeking information
inquiry	usually refers to a major question: a public inquiry into Terminal 5, for instance
sink	basin (noun) or gradually disappear (verb) and many other uses
sync	balance (comes from 'synchronicity'. The phrase is 'out of sync' meaning out of balance – I saw it written as 'out of sink' which is why it's on the list)
meter	a device to measure something, as in water meter
metre	a unit of measure

course	a series, studies, process and many other meanings
coarse	rough, rude, common
apprise	to inform (but why not use 'inform' or 'tell'?)
appraise	to estimate the value of something, evaluate someone's performance

Fourteen

Punctuation

Lynne Truss's book Eats, Shoots and Leaves was an unexpected best seller on this subject. The placing of the comma after 'eats' transforms the description of a bear's diet – eats shoots and leaves – to what sounds like the activities of a hoodlum, shoots and leaves becoming verbs rather than nouns. The joys of the English language! I'd like to think the book's popularity showed a sudden passion for punctuation amongst the British population but I haven't seen much evidence that her messages have been taken to heart. Here's a much shorter explanation of how and when to use it.

Punctuation is really important. When we speak, most of us have a certain rhythm to our speech, ups and downs, inflections and emphasis, to add meaning to what we're saying and help the listener get the message. Some people speak in a monotone but their listeners rapidly switch off – it's much too much like hard work. When you write, it's punctuation that creates the rhythm.

Punctuation helps your readers understand your message. It shows them how you want them to read what you have written. Punctuation marks are signals; they tell readers what to do and when to breathe:

- pause here
- stop here
- start again here
- take a breath!

and they give readers information:

- this group of words asks a question
- this is a quotation
- this is direct speech
- here comes a list
- this is one idea

It's your job as the writer to give your readers the right instructions and information by using the correct punctuation marks in the correct places; if you don't, they may well misinterpret your meaning. We've all had the experience of having to read a sentence several times to work out what meaning the writer intended; the cause would usually have been a lack of punctuation giving us the right signals.

Two principles govern the use of punctuation:

1. If it doesn't clarify the text, leave it out.
2. Help the reader read it right as quickly as possible.

Capital letters

First of all, let's look at when to use capital letters. Capital letters are sometimes referred to as 'upper case' – it goes back to typewriters – and 'lower case' means the letter isn't capitalised.

When to use capitals:

1. 'I' is always capitalised
2. at the beginning of a sentence
3. proper nouns: England, Roger Smith, Manchester
4. at the beginning of reported speech: He said: "Please take this."
5. for each important word in a title: 'The Left in Europe'
6. for days of the week, months of the year, festivals but not seasons – spring, summer, autumn, winter start with lower case
7. at the beginning of lines of verse
8. for words indicating rank or profession when used with the person's name: *Captain Matthews* led his company. *Judge Rook* entered the court. (**but:** The captain was a good leader. The judge made notes.)

Punctuation marks

There are two categories: major and minor. Major punctuation marks invite the reader to take a big breath. Minor ones play a lesser role but are no less important.

There are six majors:

- full stop.
- question mark ?
- exclamation mark !
- colon :
- semi colon ;
- dash –

And there are six minors:

- comma **,**
- apostrophe **'**
- hyphen **-**
- brackets **( )**
- inverted comma **'**
- quotation marks **"**

The majors

Full stop

We discussed sentences under section 6 Tips for writing clearly. The job of a sentence is to convey an idea. A full stop marks the end of a sentence. It tells the reader that you've finished one idea and it's followed by a capital letter which tells the reader you're starting a new idea. It's followed by two spaces to give the reader a chance to take a breath.

Question mark

Question marks immediately tell the reader that you're asking a question, and you need an answer. You use them after a direct question:

> *Are we to announce the results before the meeting?*
> *"Where are you going?" she asked.*
> *Can you get the information to me by Friday?*
> *Are you free to meet some time on Thursday morning?*

You don't use them after an indirect question:

> *I wonder if we should announce the results before the next meeting.*
> *She asked him where he was going.*
> *I wonder if we could meet some time on Thursday morning.*

In Spanish, they put an upside-down question mark at the beginning of the question which has always struck me as a sensible idea but it has yet to catch on in English.

Exclamation mark

Use these to:

1. indicate that a sentence is exclamatory

    My bill for that appalling meal was £40!

    If you were speaking it, you would be squeaking with indignation.

2. indicate that a word or group of words conveys a command

    'Go!'
    'Come back!'
    'Close that door!'

3. follow an interjection (see Parts of speech page 43)

    Help!
    Right!

Use exclamation marks sparingly. It's the only punctuation mark that has an underlying meaning that could be misinterpreted and cause offence. For example, if I wrote: 'Thanks for the report!' it might be a sincere thank-you but, with the exclamation mark, I might be hinting 'and about time too' or 'call that a report?' or 'are you seriously expecting me to read through all that?' Use your judgement and think about how your readers might react.

Colon

Use these to:

- introduce a list within a sentence:
  - *She decided to take a small sewing kit: scissors, thread, needles and buttons.*

- introduce a list of bullet points, all of which depend on the preceding words:

By the end of the workshop, delegates will:
  - *understand how to write clearly and concisely*
  - *have a toolkit to promote good written communication*
  - *be able to save time when writing by using their time more effectively*
  - *understand the importance of grammar and spelling*

- introduce a lengthy piece of direct speech:

When they had calmed down she said: "I can understand why you are angry. I would be angry myself. But there is nothing anyone can do about it, so you might as well face up to the facts."

- convey a direct explanation:

Only one department impressed us: the Accounts Department.

Semicolon

It's easy to remember the function of a semicolon because it's a combination of a full stop and a comma ;. It's a compromise. Use it to:

1. separate items in a list, when the items are too long to be separated by commas:

   He had a wide range of interests: planning and undertaking strenuous cycle trips all over Asia; researching and writing highly exciting, often terrifying, spy novels; composing lyrical poetry which he regularly submitted to a biannual American publication.

   You could, of course, use bullet points to separate the activities.

2. stand between parts of a sentence which could stand as separate sentences, but which are closely linked in meaning:

   She was a talented musician and could play the piano and the harp; her brother was equally talented as a sportsman and played cricket and rugby for the county.

   The text above could be expressed as two sentences, two separate ideas. But, if you intended to praise the talents of this duo, the semicolon serves the purpose of making the link between them. It conveys to the reader that you're still pursuing the same idea. You could go through life without ever using it in this way but it's an elegant little number and much-used by good writers.

Dash

It looks like a large hyphen but has a different use as a major punctuation mark. Its most common use is when you're adding another thought. It's found in literature and journalism, and is fine in personal letters. In business writing, it suggests a haphazard thought process – as if you only just thought of it – so only use it if you can't think of a more appropriate punctuation mark. You can also use it, as I've just done, as a weak bracket.

The minors

Comma

Commas tell the reader which words go together, which words to emphasise, when to take a pause and when to have a quick intake of breath. They help convey the meaning but their over-use is as bad as their under-use. It's largely a matter of style but here are some rules:

1. Commas separate the items in a list:
   She bought eggs, bread, milk and cheese.
2. Commas mark off the spoken words in direct speech:
   "Janet," she said, "was twenty minutes late for the morning meeting."
3. Commas separate the clauses in a sentence.
   Nancy, who loves all types of cooking, is an expert baker.
4. Commas mark off words which could be left out and can act like brackets in a sentence:
   Stephen Jones, the company's finance director, seemed more optimistic this month than last.
5. Commas separate parts of a sentence to avoid confusion.
   Compare these two versions:
   However much time was spent checking the engine, John was nervous.
   However, much time was spent checking the engine; John was nervous.

I remember diktats from my school days which forbade the use of commas with 'and'. That would apply in a list when the 'and' replaces the final comma but sometimes we use 'and' to expand the idea within a sentence and a comma helps the structure of the sentence. For example:

The climate was harsh enough to stimulate men to adapt natural resources to their own purposes, and mild enough for survival to be possible.

The comma before the 'and' isn't essential but I think it serves to emphasise the contrast between 'harsh enough' and 'mild enough'.

So, you have some leeway about where to use commas but don't over-do it; as commas invite the readers to take a little breath, too many will have them hyper-ventilating.

Hyphens
Use hyphens in the following:

- adjectives formed from two or more words
  a well-established principle, a little-known fact
- separating letters to help pronunciation and convey meaning:
  re-create
- to avoid ambiguity: *a little used-car/a little-used car*
- nouns formed from prepositional verbs although the tendency is to make them into one word: *build-up, clean-up*
- most words that begin with *anti* and *non*
- a sum followed by 'worth': *£500-worth of repairs*

Apostrophe

We covered this under Grammar but here it is again. Use it to:

1. show where one or more letters have been missed out:

    we've (= we have)   he'll (= he will)
    who's (= who is)   they'll (= they will)
    you'd've (= you would have) I'm (= I am)
    Mike's going (= Mike is going) she's (= she is)
    we'd (= we had)   it's (= it is)

    Such abbreviations used to be frowned upon in business writing but the chattiness of email encourages their use and they've spread into other types of writing. You have to decide whether their use is appropriate.

2. show possession. The way to get this right is to ask yourself: *'To whom or to what does it belong?'* When you have answered that question, then add 's unless the word ends in 's' when just the apostrophe is usually used:

    Mike's bike = the bike belongs to Mike.
    The car's engine = the engine belonging to the car.
    The cars' tyres = the tyres belonging to the cars.
    The children's toys = the toys belonging to the children.
    The family's pet = the pet belonging to the family.
    The families' home = the home belonging to the families.
    The girls' mother = the mother belonging to the girls.

    If the possessor has a name which ends in 's', you can either just put the apostrophe after the 's' or use 's's':

Charles' (or Charles's) house has two bedrooms.
James' (or James's) wife used to be a government advisor.

And what if the name ends in 'ss'? We have friends
with the surname 'Ross'. The plural has to be 'Rosses'
So if you want to make them possess something,
the apostrophe has to be after the final 's':

The Rosses' garden is exquisite.

The possession rule is also used to cover phrases like:

a month's holiday, five minutes' delay

This is because the meaning is similar. 'A month's
holiday' means the same as 'a holiday of a month', 'Five
minutes' delay' is the same as 'a delay of five minutes'.

Apostrophes are often used incorrectly, particularly on signs and in
advertisements. Have fun spotting them but ignore how other people use
them and follow the rules.

Brackets

Again, they have two functions:

1. to explain something: UN (United Nations). Many organisations
   have a love of using capitalised letters to avoid having to write
   out whatever it is in full. If you can actually speak it as a word,
   it's called an acronym and doesn't have to be capitalised. For
   example, Nato, Unesco, Defra. It's kindly to your readers to

explain the letters the first time you use them, and you use brackets to do it.

2. to add something to the text which isn't directly related; in this case, you must be able to delete it and the sentence will still make sense. I have a problem with this in a business context; if you're taking the trouble to write it, surely you want your readers to read it, so why put it in brackets? It's your choice.

Inverted commas

Do you remember a trend for people to speak jargon words or phrases and, as they did so, they would waggle their fingers at you in a deeply irritating way? Using inverted commas in writing can engender a similar emotion. If you put them around a word or phrase, it implies that you're using the word or phrase in an unusual way; the inverted commas will somehow help the reader understand your subtle meaning. It's always a gamble so only use them if you're really sure they're needed and will help clarify exactly what you mean. For example, in a letter to a customer, a water company wrote:

'The problem is you live in an area of 'hard' water.'

My feeling is that either the customers understand the concept of hard water so the inverted commas aren't needed, or they don't, in which case they will be none the wiser without a further explanation.

That quote from the letter illustrates the other use of inverted commas: when you're quoting from a letter or report, or you want to highlight something for the reader as I did with: 'What if the name ends in 'ss'?'.

We used to put inverted commas around titles of books or newspapers but that's rather fallen out of fashion; the capital letters will do the job for us, as in The Guardian, The Daily Telegraph.

Quotation marks

That's the double hit: "Ouch!" she cried. The double ones are reserved for actual speech. Their use in business writing will probably only be when you want to record the words someone spoke. Their use is far more frequent in journalism, literature and the police force when they record the words used by a witness.

Fifteen

Spelling

Let me reiterate what I said at the beginning: this book is about writing at work. If you've developed some clever spelling for texting, twittering or other social media, that's fine but don't use them at work.

Does spelling matter? Of course it does! You're asking your readers to invest their time in reading your words; it's only courteous to minimise their effort by spelling the words correctly. And if you make spelling mistakes, they will undermine your reputation and that of your company and reduce your influence. Even people who can't spell well have a remarkable knack of being able to spot other people's mistakes.

Under no circumstances rely on spellcheck. It's a great help so please use it but don't rely on it. Spellcheck can't understand the context, it can't tell the difference between form and from, fro and for, advice and advise, their and there, here and hear. An organisation with whom I work often needs to use the word 'borehole'; spellcheck prefers 'brothel'.............And one time I was editing a document which had a sentence starting 'The *treat* of this approach ....'; the writer meant 'threat'.

You've probably all seen the text below that does the rounds on email every few years.

I cdnuolt blveiee that I cluod aulaclty uesdnatnrd what I was rdanieg. The phaonmneal pweor of the hmuan mnid, aoccdrnig to rscheearch at Cmabrigde Uinervtisy, it dseno't mtaetr in what oerdr the ltteres in a word are, the olny iproamtnt tihng is that the frsit and last ltteer be in the rghit pclae. The rset can be a taotl mses and you can still raed it whotuit a pboerlm. This is bcuseae the huamn mnid deos not raed ervey lteter by istlef, but the word as a wlohe. Azanmig huh? I awlyas tghuhot slpeling was ipmorantt!

Yes, it is amazing that our brains can unravel the meaning with just the first and last letter being correct and the number of letters in each word being accurate. But that doesn't mean we should dive into dyslexia. Correct spelling helps get the message across.

Reading helps to develop the ability to spell, as does checking in a dictionary – although that can be time-consuming if you really don't know how to spell the word. But some rules exist to help us spell correctly. First let's look at how words are made up.

Prefixes and suffixes

When you think about the meaning of a word, how it's put together will often give you a clue. Many words are made up of the stem of the word with either a *prefix* or a *suffix*, and sometimes both. A prefix is added to the beginning of the word, a suffix is added to the end.

stem	addition	equals
continue	dis	discontinue

estimate	under	underestimate
slow	ly	slowly
motion	less	motionless

The prefixes and suffixes have their own meanings.

suffix	meaning	examples
able, ible	capable of being	eatable, edible, recognisable
ian, an	connected with	parliamentarian, publican, magician
ance, ence	state of	remembrance, resemblance,
ant	one who	assistant, servant,
et, ette	little	casket, owlet, cigarette
er, eer, ier	one who	joiner, engineer, carrier
ess	female	mistress, princess, waitress
ful	full of	plentiful, meaningful, beautiful
hood	state of being	childhood, knighthood,
fy	to make	beautify, purify, simplify
less	without	careless, hopeless
ling	little	codling, gosling, yearling
ment	state of	contentment, enjoyment, resentment
ock	little	hillock, tussock
ory	a place for	dormitory, factory, priory
ous	full of	courageous, famous, glorious

Prefix	meaning	examples
a	on	aboard, afloat, ashore
a, ab, abs	away, from	avert, abdicate, absent
ad, ac	to	admit, accept, accede

ante	before	antecedent, anteroom
anti	opposite, against	antibiotic, antidote
bi, bis	two, twice	bicycle, bigamy, biscuit
circum	round	circumference, circumvent
con, com	together	connect, compete, convene
contra	against	contradict, contrary
de	down	descend, depress, decline
dis	away, not	discharge, disappear, disagree
ex	a) out of	extract, export, excursion
	b) formerly, before	ex-Prime Minister
fore	previous	forecast, foretell, foresee
im, in	a) in, into	import, incision, include
	b) not	immovable, impractical, incapable, incorrect
inter	between	international, interval, intervene
mis	wrong, wrongly	misconduct, mischief, misbehave
ob	a) open, clear	obvious, observe
	b) against	obstruct, object, obstacle
post	after	postpone, postscript, post meridian (pm = afternoon)
pro	a) in front of	proceed, progress, propeller
	b) in favour of	profess, prophet, propose
re	a) again	reappear, retake, repeat
	b) back	return, retrace, rebate
sub	under	submarine, subway, subsonic
super	over, beyond	superior, superhuman
trans	across	transfer, transport,
un	not	unimportant, unsafe, untrue
vice	acting for	vice-captain, vice-admiral, viceroy

Now for the rules. Just a quick reminder: with letters of the alphabet, a, e, i, o and u are called vowels; all the others are called consonants. 'Syllable' refers to the spoken divisions in the word: word has one syllable, di-vis-ions has three.

1. **Never add or subtract a letter when joining a prefix**

mis + inform	=	misinform
mis + shape	=	misshape
with + hold	=	withhold

    There are no exceptions to this rule.

2. **i before e except after c when the sound is eee:**

    achieve, believe, chief, field, ceiling, receive, hygiene

    exception: seize

    When the sound is not **eee** you have to remember which is correct.

tied	tried	lied	friend
eight	height	rein	their
leisure			

3. **When adding to a word which ends with a consonant + y, change the y to i unless the addition begins with i (eg 'ing'):**

baby	babies	jelly	jellies
city	cities	country	countries
try	tries	try	trying
fly	flies	fly	flying

4. When adding to a word which ends with a vowel + y keep the y:

monkey	monkeys	play	player
annoy	annoys	pay	payable

exceptions

daily	said	laid	paid

5. When adding -ing to a word which ends with <u>e</u>, drop the <u>e</u> then add -ing

acquire	acquiring	come	coming
declare	declaring	cycle	cycling
suppose	supposing	promise	promising

exceptions: singe   singeing   (otherwise it would be singing) and when there is a vowel before the last e

see	seeing	canoe	canoeing

6. When adding to a word which ends with e, keep the e when the addition begins with a consonant:

like	likewise	rare	rarely
advance	advancement	definite	definitely

exceptions:

argue	+	ment	argument
due	+	ly	duly

| true | + | ly | truly |
| whole | + | ly | wholly |

7. **When adding the suffixes 'able' or 'ous' to a word ending ge or ce, keep the e to preserve the soft sound of the c and g:**

| courage | + | ous | courageous |
| notice | + | able | noticeable |

8. **When adding a suffix which begins with a vowel to a word ending with a consonant, double the consonant when:**

a) **the word is a single syllable**

| shop | shopping | thin | thinner |
| plan | planned | blot | blotting |

b) **the word is two syllables and the final syllable is stressed**

| prefer | preferring | begin | beginning |
| forgot | forgotten | refer | referred |

This is to do with how we pronounce the words. We emphasise the 'fer' in the word 'refer'. If you emphasise the 're' it means something quite different.

c) **the word ends in L**

cancel	cancelled
travel	travelled
unravel	unravelled

9. Don't double the final consonant when:

a) **the last syllable is not stressed**

visit	visiting
listen	listening
focus	focusing
target	targeted
budget	budgeting

b) **the word ends in two consonants**

thick	thickest
turn	turned

c) **the word has two vowels before the final consonant**

boil	boiled
need	needing

10. *c*   words are nouns
   s   words are verbs

We discussed this under section13 Words which cause confusion.

noun	*verb*
advice	advise
licence	license
practice	practise
device	devise

11. When full or fill is joined to a word it drops one L

care-full = careful
rest-full = restful

12. When full is joined to a word which ends with double LL, *both* words drop one L

full + fill = fulfil
skill + full = skilful

13. Plurals

Most words ending with **ch, sh, ss, x add es**

eg   church   churches
      pouch   pouches
      ditch   ditches
      match   matches
      rush   rushes
      dish   dishes
      dress   dresses
      class   classes
      box   boxes
      wax   waxes
      fox   foxes

Most words ending with **o** add **es**

potato	potatoes
hero	heroes
tomato	tomatoes

exceptions: solos   pianos   studios

Words ending in a consonant + y, change y to i and add es (Rule 3)

robbery	robberies	memory	memories
country	countries	pony	ponies

Words ending in a vowel + y, keep y and add s (Rule 4)

boy	boys	donkey	donkeys
day	days	journey	journeys

Here's a poem which highlights the impossibility of producing rules about how to pronounce English words. The author is anonymous so sadly we can't acknowledge the genius who wrote it. Try reading it out loud – to give you a clue, it's written in rhyming couplets.

I take it you already know
Of tough and bough and cough and dough?
Others may stumble but not you,
On hiccough, thorough, laugh and through .....
Well done! And now you wish, perhaps,
To learn of less familiar traps.

Beware of heard: a dreadful word
That looks like beard and sounds like bird.
And dead: it's said like bed not bead –
For goodness sake don't call it deed.

Watch out for meat and great and threat
(They rhyme with suite and straight and debt!)
A moth is not a moth in mother;
Nor both in bother, broth in brother;

And here is not a match for there,
Nor dear and fear for bear and pear.
And then there's dose and rose and lose
(Just look them up) and goose and choose,
And cork and work and card and ward,
And font and front and word and sword,

And do and go and thwart and cart .....
Come, come! I've hardly made a start.

A dreadful language? Man alive!
I'd mastered it when I was five!

I will teach you in my verse
Words like corps, corks, hose and worse,
For this phonetic labyrinth
Gives monkey, donkey, ninth and plinth,
Wounded, rounded, grieve and sieve,
Friend and fiend, alive and live.

Query does not rhyme with very,
Nor does fury sound like bury.
Dies and diet, lord and word,
Earth and hearth and clerk and herd;

Evil, devil, tomb, bomb, comb;
Doll and roll, dull, bull, some and home.
Finally – for I've said enough –
Through though thorough plough cough tough
While hiccough has the sound of cup .....
My advice is: give it up!

We can't, of course, give it up. But, if English is your mother tongue,
thank your lucky stars!

Sixteen

Checklist for writing and editing

Here's a summary of what we've covered to help you when you're writing or when you're editing text written by someone else. The editing role is a sensitive one; there's a great temptation to change things, if only to prove you're doing your job. Resist the temptation to make any changes that aren't firmly based on the rules of good writing and be prepared to explain them to the writer.

First impressions

- easy to read – font size, margins, white space
- shapely text – left-justified only
- good use of headings and bullet points
- no huge chunks of text

Structure and logic

- grabs the reader's attention
- instant relevance – aha! this is what it's about
- most important information upfront

- easy to scan – signpost sentences to introduce each paragraph
- no paragraph more than six sentences
- action points on first page

Sentences

- average no more than 20 words in each sentence
- good use of punctuation
- active voice
- no ambiguity – no need to read a sentence more than once

Words

- maximum 10% long words: words of three syll-a-bles or more
- strong language – no waffle
- no padding – every word helps the reader understand
- familiar to the reader
- all acronyms explained first time they're used

Perfection! If it's important, get someone else to check it – you can't see your own mistakes.

- no typos
- no spelling mistakes
- no misuse of words
- no glitches on graphics

Exercises

Here are some exercises to help you consolidate what we've covered. The solutions are at the back.

Mistakes

There are 29 separate mistakes in the sentences below – they could be to do with grammar or spelling.

1. Anglers' must have rod licenses.

2. Companies plans for conserving water is contained in water resource plans.

3. If they practice each day they'll become skillfull.

4. Each of the books have a stain on their covers.

5. Outside of the agency's concerned, there's little concensus on the way foreward.

6. Their are less people practicing religion these day's.

7. The agency is a licencing authority and proscribes certain proceedures.

8. Its reccommended in the advise manual to follow it's instructions closely.

9. The meeting focussed on problems between the department and yourself.

10. The currant in the river increases in Winter.

Apostrophes

1. We fully support the Mayors decision to publish a strategy.

2. Londons economic prosperity has created todays problems.

3. Customers needs must be taken into account.

4. Any development should respect these sites designations and permission will not be granted for any development that will negatively affect them.

5. Its a shame the company lost its chief executive when it did.

6. The organisations systems take account of its duties and powers in considering whether to grant new licences.

7. The strategy aims to recognise both abstractors reasonable needs for water and environmental needs.

8. The principles are to protect other legitimate river users interests.

9. A childs chromosomes are an irretrievably scrambled mishmash of its grandparents chromosomes and so on back to distant ancestors.

10. Theres going to be a sale of boys and mens clothing in a weeks time.

11. Cherry blossom is a glorious sign of springs arrival.

Affect/effect

1. The (affect/effect) of this pollution will last for many years.

2. Sunshine (affects/effects) the way we see things.

3. The hot weather has badly (affected/effected) fish populations in our rivers.

4. His health was (affected/effected) by hours spent gazing at a computer screen.

5. The surge in algae has had a disastrous (affect/effect) on fish.

6. Staff morale will be (affected/effected) by the pay award.

7. This could have one of three (affects/effects).

8. The Charges Scheme will put into (affect/effect) the changes required by the Water Bill.

Pronouns

Use the correct pronouns below; you might have to change the order of words.

1. Who has the report been sent to?

2. Please send the information to myself.

3. They are the experts in the teams they are involved with.

4. Myself and Carol will be going to the conference.

5. Who's pen is this?

6. Her and him share a house in the country.

7. I chaired the meeting on behalf of himself who was on holiday.

8. Them and us had an interesting discussion after herself left the room.

9. The man who I saw walking across the road tripped and fell in front of the bus.

10. He said that her and me presented the best argument for leaving things as they are.

11. They're use of mobile phones interrupted the meeting.

12. Stephen and me have a great understanding about what matters.

Which is the correct word?

1. I need your (advice/advise) on this report.

2. Will the embargo have any (affect/effect) on medical supplies?

3. The Environment Agency is the (licencing/licensing) authority and issues (licences/licenses).

4. He (lead/led) his horse over the damaged bridge.

5. During the (passed/past) six months, his boss has been impossible.

6. If your tie is (lose/loose) you may (lose/loose) out at the interview.

7. If you (practice/practise) every day, the (practice/practise) will make you perfect.

8. If you sit (quite/quiet) still you can (hear/here) the river.

9. We must allow (to/too/two) hours for the journey (to/too/two) London so we don't arrive (to/too/two) late for dinner.

10. Jane and (I/me) can take you in the car if you speak to (she/her) first.

11. If you explain the situation to David and (I/me), we might be able to make allowances.

12. (Whose/who's) coming to the meeting next Friday?

13. The person (who's/whose) car is parked outside the building must move it immediately.

14. The writer (who/whom) you admire is speaking at the Book Festival.

15. The manager (who/whom) always asks difficult questions is leaving at the end of the month.

Punctuation and capital letters

I've removed all the punctuation and capital letters from the three paragraphs below. Have a go at punctuating them and adding the capital letters, bearing in mind that the aim is to help the reader understand the message at first reading. You may punctuate them differently from the original writers; that doesn't necessarily make your version wrong but compare the differences.

1. when i got married 50 fifty years ago my wife and i had somehow acquired a little cookery book called cooking in ten mnutes we never quite managed to cook anything in so short a time mainly i think because the book was a bit of a cheat it seemed to expect you to have a saucepan full of boiling water and a whole lot of washed and prepared vegetables ready before the ten minutes began we lost the book long ago but 40 years afterwards i read a volume of essays by julian barnes the pedant in the kitchen in which he devoted an entire chapter to french cooking in ten minutes and to its author edouard de pomiane who he informed me had been a food scientist and dietician much admired by elizabeth david

2. unlike almost everyone i know i was always very fond of the staple school puddings of my childhood rice pudding semolina and anything with custard all of them nicer with skin on the top i was inspired by these dishes to find their grownup equivalents which are generally better cooked so now i eschew birds custard but love the real thing on easter day my niece anna who like many teenagers today is a brilliant pastry cook produced an italian dish called pastiera napoletana di grano sometimes known as easter pie its whole boiled wheat grains symbolise new life concealed cooked in ricotta these grains had a taste which gave me a proustian recall of my favourite school pudding tapioca the revival of interest in nursery food is deserved not merely because of this nostalgia effect but because it is really more exciting than people noticed at the time

3. this failure north of the border reflects a broader failure to persuade people that britain has a bright future fifty four per cent of britons think that young peoples lives will be worse than those of their parents generation according to a recent poll only one in five say they will be better this majority pessimism helps explain why ukip is doing so well as one conservative minister laments ukip has captured a zeitgeist of grumpiness if you believe that things are going to get worse whoever is in government why not vote for the party that expresses your anger about this most vigorously

Active and passive voice

Scientists are notorious for using the passive voice; their academic training is to blame. See what you can do to translate this into the active voice – remember the syntax: subject, verb, object ....

Magic sponge

Sea creatures could be a goldmine for powerful drugs

It is claimed by researchers in Florida that self defence chemicals produced by a sponge could be used as anti fungal drugs. It is hoped that the chemicals could be used against the growing army of drug resistant infections.

The seas were scoured for new anti fungal drugs by Peter McCarthy of Harbor Branch Oceanographic Institution in Florida. Sponges and other invertebrates were collected from waters down to depths of 1 kilometre.

Samples were identified and chemical extracts prepared by McCarthy and his team which were sent to Denver based company Mycologics to be analysed. The extracts were tested on two notorious pathogens: *Candida albicans (Ca)* and *Aspergillus fumigatus (Af)*. Skin infections and thrush are caused by *Ca* and dangerous lung infections in people with weakened immune systems by *Af.*

After 3500 extracts had been screened,101 interesting candidates were identified by Mycologics. A completely new class of anti fungal agents called cyclic peroxy acids were considered to be the most promising; they act differently from many anti fungals and both species in the test tube were killed off by them. The compounds are made by an animal – *Plakinistrella* – an unassuming black sponge that inhabits the seas off the Seychelles.

The efficacity and toxicity of the compounds in people has yet to be measured by the team. However, McCarthy says that it is a rare and valuable insight to have spotted a new Achilles' heel in fungi.

Solutions

Mistakes

1. Anglers must have rod licences. (The plural of Anglers doesn't need an apostrophe and the noun 'licence' has a 'c' at the end)

2. Companies' plans for conserving water are contained in water resource plans. (The sentence means 'plans of the companies' so companies needs an apostrophe, and the plans are plural so it has to be 'are' not 'is')

3. If they practise each day they'll become skilful. (Practise is a verb so needs an 's' not a 'c', and when skill – full becomes one word, you drop one 'l' from each word)

4. Each of the books has a stain on its cover. (Each means 'every one of' so it has to be singular, the verb has to agree as does the possessive pronoun 'its')

5. Outside the agencies concerned, there's little consensus on the way forward. (Outside should never be followed by 'of', the plural of agency is agencies, consensus comes from the verb ' to consent' and forward has no 'e', unlike 'foreword' which means an introduction)

6. There are fewer people practising religion these days. (They're pronounced the same but 'their' is the possessive pronoun of they, it should be fewer because you can count them, practising is part of the verb so has an 's' and the plural of 'days' doesn't need an apostrophe)

7. The Agency is a licensing authority and prescribes certain procedures. (You probably need a capital A for Agency, licensing is part of the verb so needs an 's', proscribes means to prohibit whereas the sentence means 'prescribes', imposes, and procedures doesn't have a double ee)

8. It's recommended in the advice manual to follow its instructions closely. (Its needs an apostrophe for the sentence to make sense, recommended doesn't have a double cc, advice is being used as a noun so needs a 'c' and the last 'its' is the possessive pronoun so doesn't need an apostrophe)

9. The meeting focused on problems between the department and you. (Focused doesn't take a double ss because we stress the first syllable, and you is the correct pronoun)

10. The current in the river increases in winter. (They sound the same but current is the correct word, not a piece of dried fruit, and the seasons never start with a capital letter)

Apostrophes

1. We fully support the Mayor's decision to publish a strategy.

2. London's economic prosperity has created today's problems.

3. Customers' needs must be taken into account.

4. Any development should respect these sites' designations and permission will not be granted for any development that will negatively affect them.

5. It's a shame the company lost its chief executive when it did.

6. The organisation's systems take account of its duties and powers in considering whether to grant new licences.

7. The strategy aims to recognise both abstractors' reasonable needs for water and environmental needs.

8. The principles are to protect other legitimate river users' interests.

9. A child's chromosomes are an irretrievably scrambled mishmash of its grandparents' chromosomes and so on back to distant ancestors.

10. There's going to be a sale of boys' and men's clothing in a week's time.

11. Cherry blossom is a glorious sign of spring's arrival.

Affect/effect

1. The effect of this pollution will last for many years.

2. Sunshine affects the way we see things.

3. The hot weather has badly affected fish populations in our rivers.

4. His health was affected by hours spent gazing at a computer screen.

5. The surge in algae has had a disastrous effect on fish.

6. Staff morale will be affected by the pay award.

7. This could have one of three effects.

8. The Charges Scheme will put into effect the changes required by the Water Bill.

Pronouns

1. To whom has the report been sent?

2. Please send the information to me.

3. They are the experts in the teams with whom they are involved.

4. Carol and I will be going to the conference.

5. Whose pen is this?

6. She and he share a house in the country.

7. I chaired the meeting on behalf of the person who was on holiday.

8. They and we had an interesting discussion after she left the room.

9. The man whom I saw walking across the road tripped and fell in front of the bus.

10. He said that she and I presented the best argument for leaving things as they are.

11. Their use of mobile phones interrupted the meeting.

12. Stephen and I have a great understanding about what matters.

Which is the correct word?

1. I need your advice on this report.

2. Will the embargo have any effect on medical supplies?

3. The Environment Agency is the licensing authority and issues licences.

4. He led his horse over the damaged bridge.

5. During the past six months, his boss has been impossible.

6. If your tie is loose you may lose out at the interview.

7. If you practise every day, the practice will make you perfect.

8. If you sit quite still you can hear the river.

9. We must allow two hours for the journey to London so we don't arrive too late for dinner.

10. Jane and I can take you in the car if you speak to her first.

11. If you explain the situation to David and me, we might be able to make allowances.

12. Who's coming to the meeting next Friday?

13. The person whose car is parked outside the building must move it immediately.

14. The writer whom you admire is speaking at the Book Festival.

15. The manager who always asks difficult questions is leaving at the end of the month.

Punctuation and capitals

There's always some choice in the use of punctuation but this is how the writers punctuated the originals.

1. When I got married 50 fifty years ago, my wife and I had somehow acquired a little cookery book called Cooking in Ten Minutes. We never quite managed to cook anything in so short a time, mainly, I think, because the book was a bit of a cheat; it seemed to expect you to have a saucepan full of boiling water and a whole lot of washed and prepared vegetables ready before the ten minutes began. We lost the book long ago, but 40 years afterwards I read a volume of essays by Julian Barnes, The Pedant in the Kitchen, in which he devoted an entire chapter to French Cooking in Ten Minutes and to its author, Edouard de Pomiane, who, he informed me, had been a food scientist and dietician much admired by Elizabeth David.

2. Unlike almost everyone I know, I was always very fond of the staple school puddings of my childhood – rice pudding, semolina and anything with custard (all of them nicer with skin on the top). I was inspired by these dishes to find their grown-up

equivalents which are generally better cooked; so now I eschew Bird's custard but love the real thing. On Easter day, my niece Anna, who like many teenagers today is a brilliant pastry cook, produced an Italian dish called pastiera napoletana di grano sometimes known as 'Easter pie'. Its whole boiled wheat grains symbolise new life concealed. Cooked in ricotta, these grains had a taste which gave me a Proustian recall of my favourite school pudding, tapioca. The revival of interest in 'nursery food' is deserved, not merely because of this nostalgia effect but because it is really more exciting than people noticed at the time.

3. This failure north of the border reflects a broader failure to persuade people that Britain has a bright future. Fifty four per cent of Britons think that young people's lives will be worse than those of their parents' generation according to a recent poll. Only one in five say they will be better. This majority pessimism helps explain why Ukip is doing so well. As one Conservative minister laments, "Ukip has captured a zeitgeist of grumpiness." If you believe that things are going to get worse whoever is in government, why not vote for the party that expresses your anger about this most vigorously?

Magic sponge – using the active voice

Sea creatures could be a goldmine for powerful drugs

Self-defence chemicals produced by a sponge could work as anti-fungal drugs, say researchers in Florida. They hope the chemicals could be used against the growing army of drug-resistant infections.

Peter McCarthy of Harbor Branch Oceanographic Institution in Florida and his team scoured the seas for new anti-fungal drugs. They collected samples of sponges and other invertebrates from waters down to depths of 1 kilometre.

After identifying the samples, McCarthy and his team prepared chemical extracts which they sent to Denver-based company Mycologics for analysis. The extracts were tested on two notorious human pathogens:*Candida albican*, which causes skin infections and thrush, and *Aspergillus fumigatus*, which causes dangerous lung infections in people with weakened immune systems.

After screening more than 3500 extracts, Mycologics identified 101 interesting candidates. The most promising of these were a completely new class of anti-fungal agents called cyclic peroxy acids, which killed off both species in the test tube and act differently from many anti-fungals. The animal that makes the compounds is *Plakinistrella*, an unassuming black sponge that lives in the seas off the Seychelles.

The team has yet to measure the efficacy and toxicity of the compounds in people but McCarthy says that spotting a new Achilles' heel in fungi is a rare and valuable insight.

57477161R00097

Made in the USA
Charleston, SC
18 June 2016